GYPSY
From Koh Samui to Bollington

Bob Cooper

ISBN: 978-1-916732-51-3

Copyright 2025

All rights reserved. No part of this publication may be reproduced, stored in a retrieval system, or transmitted in any form or by any means, electronic, mechanical, photocopy, recording or otherwise, without prior written consent of the copyright owner. Nor can it be circulated in any form of binding or cover other than that in which it is published and without similar condition including this condition being imposed on a subsequent purchaser. The right of Bob Cooper to be identified as the author of this work has been asserted in accordance with the Copyright Designs and Patents Act 1988. A copy of this book is deposited with the British Library.

Published by:

www.i2ipublishing.co.uk

i2i Publishing, Manchester.

In loving memory of Phil Keggin,
who shared this amazing
life changing experience with me.

Contents

Arrival in Thailand 1

Chaweng Beach and the DRCS 7

Koh Samui Night Life 15

Return To Koh Samui 23

Heartbreak Hotel! 33

Third Time Lucky? 45

The Songkran Festival 53

Surprise Reunion 79

What Next for Gypsy? 85

Life-Changing Decision 93

Success at Last 103

Back Home Again 109

Gypsy in Quarantine 117

Living in Bollington 141

Tsunami! 155

Friends of Doris Day 165

What a Coincidence! 173

Come Fly with Me! 181

Arrival in Thailand

'Whatever were we thinking of?'

Koh Samui is a Thai island paradise situated in the South China Sea and is one of over forty different islands in the Ang Thong Marine Park. Only seven of them are inhabited and it is the third largest and translates as the 'golden basin'. It was the favourite destination for backpackers from the early eighties onwards. Some of those very same people would be appalled at how much the island has developed since then, based on it becoming a highly popular tourist destination. We had decided to tackle another long-haul flight since flying to Goa a couple of years earlier. We booked a holiday to Thailand and little did we know how much that decision would affect our lives in the coming years. 'Koh' is the Thai word for island, incidentally.

Through my work as a professional video cameraman filming mostly weddings and special family occasions, but also theatre productions and sporting events, it was becoming increasingly difficult to fit in a foreign holiday. My busiest months from a wedding point of view, were between March and October so it ruled out going to Mediterranean and European destinations more and more. Because of that, Phil and I made the decision to spread our wings and travel further afield outside of those months. The Gambia, Goa, Barbados and Kenya were the initial four long-haul destinations we visited, till eventually we became even more adventurous by deciding to fly further east and visit Thailand.

During the course of our holiday jaunts we experienced so many diverse adventures like accidentally gate-crashing a Russian Christmas party in Riga! We were robbed in the street in Barbados on another holiday and also went by taxi to the top of the Atlas Mountains in Morocco as one normally does!! It only cost about £112 and no, it wasn't with Silvertown Taxis! We even had a conversation with Goldie Hawn in the sea at Mandraki beach on Skiathos! These unusual incidents pale into insignificance based on the story we are about to unveil regarding our Thai adventures!

Some background with regard to Phil: For many years he had small roles working in TV after gaining B.A. Honours and M.A. degrees in creative arts as well as writing. He regularly appeared in Coronation Street, Emmerdale, Heartbeat, Brookside, Peak Practice, Boon and many others, even twice in Prime Suspect including an important scene with Helen Mirren. I also did a few appearances with him, but we both played conservative MPs in the film 'Scandal', which starred Ian McKellen (before he was knighted) as John Profumo in 1989. There is a very brief shot of us in a scene from the film in the Dusty Springfield video 'Nothing Has Been Proved' written by Pet Shop Boys, which played over the closing credits! One of our proudest moments!

The most bizarre production we worked on together was a Welsh language TV film called 'Brad' in which we played two of Adolf Hitler's henchmen in uniform, in temperatures touching the nineties! Under the circumstances, not an ideal situation! Particularly when I developed a severe migraine due to a tight cap worn in that excessive heat. The producer complained that I was costing HTV a lot of money waiting for me to recover! What a nuisance I was! After a break of half an hour we resumed filming. Unfortunately, we could only watch a very snowy version when it was televised as it was transmitted via Harlech TV in Wales and the reception was so poor where we lived in Cheshire! All we could see were blurred shadowy figures moving about the screen and we could not understand the language either!

In January 1998 we flew to Bangkok with Thai Airways, which included a two hour stop in Dubai, on what seemed like a never-ending journey. We spent that time wandering around the unbelievably large duty-free area till we resumed our ongoing flight. We were beginning to ask ourselves 'whatever were we thinking of?' Once we were in Bangkok's massive airport, after a wait of two hours, we transferred onto a Bangkok Airways flight to Koh Samui, which took approximately fifty-five minutes. It was a small plane seating only 40 passengers and we all had to be weighed before boarding so they could balance both sides of the plane! Thankfully, we didn't fall into the heavyweight bracket!

On this flight I was sitting next to a young woman who was a lone traveller. I was surprised to learn her age was only 18, and I told her she was very brave to travel somewhere like Thailand on her own. She explained that she was meeting three members of her family who had been there for two weeks already. For her, this was an explorative visit prior to going on a backpacking holiday with several college friends when they finished university the following year. She suggested we could perhaps meet up while we were all there so she told us the hotel they were staying in. This was close to the centre of Chaweng, not too far from our own. We made a tentative arrangement for 8pm two days later and had the most wonderful evening with these new friends. They kept in touch with us for some time afterwards. Clare fell in love with Thailand and continued to take other holidays there, including Chang Mai once, which is somewhere we never managed to visit.

Flying above the group of different islands en route was so breathtaking as they each came into view. After we landed in Koh Samui, we were astonished to see the modes of transport taking us from the plane to the arrival suite. They were like mini open-topped train carriages painted intricately with multicoloured flowers, palm trees and butterflies. They were totally unique, as was the airport lounge which was covered with a thatched roof. Otherworldly is the word I am looking for. Moments like this made us realise just why we had made the decision to be airborne for so many hours. From then on, the long journeys in the future never crossed our minds, as we knew there was a rainbow and a pot of gold at the end of it!

After we became acclimatised on this first holiday there, we realised that for the dog community, it was the exact opposite to paradise. Most of the dogs on the island spent their precarious lives on the beach or wandering the busy streets of the towns and villages. Most had not been vaccinated, and all were able to breed and are left to frequently become involved in horrendous fights that break out. The majority of them were open to all canine diseases including rabies, though this had more or less been eradicated. Skin disorders were rife and often weeping sores and severe loss of coat prevented the dogs from gaining the attention of the tourists they depend on. Those dogs that ventured onto the streets to forage for food or to sleep in shop doorways, often faced untimely deaths from the volume of traffic passing through the town. After the restaurants had closed it was commonplace to witness dogs frantically clawing open refuse bags for something to eat. This is when a few unscrupulous hotel owners took the opportunity to bury poisoned meat inside the bags with the intention of eliminating the canine population.

Chaweng Beach and the DRCS

'A proper functioning dog clinic was the ultimate goal'

After our first walk along Chaweng's main beach, we became aware of just how many dogs were in need of feeding and we decided we had to try and do something about it. Some of them were so thin and emaciated, they could barely stand upright. Phil and I were able to buy bags of complete dog food and biscuits from the only supermarket in the main tourist resort, so we could at least give as many dogs as possible some decent food to eat. Having three dogs ourselves at home in England at that time made us feel it was our responsibility to help as many of the Thai dogs as we could in the two weeks we were there.

My first connection with dogs goes back to when I was eight years old when I lived in Everton valley, a very poor and rundown part of Liverpool. Our very first family pet was a dog we called Prince. It was being attacked viciously by two other dogs in front of our house, so I persuaded my mother to let us take it in for a couple of days. Of course it ended up staying much longer than that, as I became very attached to it. Unfortunately, my parents did not, as he was very destructive around the house when he was left on his own. The final straw was when we returned home one day after shopping, to find Prince had completely destroyed half the sofa and the carpet was covered in horse hair! Two days later, after I arrived home from school, he was nowhere to be seen. My mother told me that she was sorry but we could not have kept him any longer because of his destructive behaviour. They had him put to sleep and the bottom fell right out of my world and I was heartbroken for months.

About a year later, on a visit to Southampton to see my father's relatives, I became attached to a collie puppy that was part of a litter. We brought her back to Liverpool and called her Lassie like the famous film dog and thankfully she turned out to be very gentle and obedient. After she passed away there was a long gap without dogs as I lived in a series of flats and was not permitted to own any.

The gateway to my extensive worldwide travel exploits was opened in my teens when I decided to go on my own to the continent by rail and boat. I visited Belgium, Holland, France and Germany much against my mother's wishes and I enjoyed it so much. I needed to break out of the rut our family was in by going down to Southampton to see my father's relatives every year. Since then, I have visited over sixty-five different countries and each year I still try to add a new one.

In the seventies and eighties I was employed by Arrowsmith Holidays in Liverpool, a northern subsidiary of Laker Airways, home of Skytrain. Unfortunately, Freddie's company folded in 1985 but our branch was bought by Greenall Whitley, the brewery, and eventually the business was transferred to Manchester, overlooking Piccadilly Gardens. On the day the takeover was announced, the office was turned into a temporary bar and the staff enjoyed socialising with the new owners. It was a huge news story, so the BBC and ITV cameras came onto the premises to cover it. I have the most amazing memory of the 10pm ITV News starting with the usual Big Ben image and dramatic theme music and there was myself and Jennie, one of my staff, posing with two beers as we were briefly interviewed. My 20 seconds of fame!! We were also featured on BBC television the same night.

For roughly seven months we were bussed from Liverpool to Manchester till the number of staff gradually lessened and it became unsustainable for the company to keep this arrangement going. I was then encouraged to move to the new office or resign from my job, so I reluctantly chose the former and Greenall's were quite generous with moving expenses. It was an ideal time in many ways as both of Phil's parents had passed away in the same year and he was unhappy in his current job. He started in a new travel agency simultaneously in Manchester's city centre and we acquired a house in Bredbury, Stockport. We then commuted to Manchester on a twenty-minute train journey. This is when a long relationship with dogs began as it enabled us to rescue a dog from North Manchester Dog's Home who we named Dusty after my favourite singer Dusty Springfield. I think it must have been the kohl black eyelashes!

I was thrilled at once again being able to own a dog, but we received a huge shock when four weeks later she gave birth to a litter of five pups! This was on the day before travelling to Amsterdam for a long weekend break! Luckily, our next door neighbour Warwick looked after them while we were away. They all opened their eyes on Christmas day so that was an unexpected present. Over the next couple of months we found owners for three of them, one being a young lady called Moira Buffini. We became close friends and eventually she established herself as a famous playwright and actor and has written and appeared in many plays. Two were adapted into the films 'Tamara Drew' and 'Byzantium'. I also filmed Moira's wedding in Chester some years later. Being unable to find homes for the remaining two pups, we then became the proud owners of three dogs! Dusty, Heidi and Hero.

My career at Arrowsmith ended three years after moving to the new office and I was made redundant! I joined an employment agency and proceeded to do a variety of part-time work while at the same time building up my job as a freelance video cameraman, which I have been ever since. In hindsight it was the best career decision I ever made.

In Koh Samui, the idea of a dog rescue centre originated from Danny van Urk from the Netherlands in 1997, who Brigitte Gomm became acquainted with on the beach one day through their mutual involvement in the dog situation. Although Danny did her best, without a vet there was only a limited amount that could be achieved. Brigitte and her husband Werner, both from Berlin, started to help realise Danny's dream by contacting all animal friends they had met during their work. Through sponsorship and donations, on April 1st, 1999, the Dog Rescue Centre Samui (DRCS) opened its doors in a converted shop, which was formerly a launderette, I believe, near the Marine Bungalows and Samui Hospital. A proper functioning dog clinic was the ultimate goal, but it was a few years later before that dream was realised. On this holiday in Thailand we were unaware of all this till the following year.

We were staying in the Novotel Mercure hotel, which was a few minutes' drive from the centre of Chaweng. A courtesy bus frequently ferried the guests back and forth to the beach and main part of town, as it was quite a considerable distance to walk. After travelling to the airport to say goodbye to some friends we had made from Cork, we arrived back at our hotel just as an extremely violent storm materialised, which caused a massive power cut in the area.

On returning to our hotel room, we showered and changed in candlelight and decided to start strolling into town, as the hotel transport had already departed. It was pitch black and all we could see was a row of very distant lights in the area where we were heading. All of a sudden, the road in front of us became brightly lit up by an approaching car's headlights. Just two steps away from me, for a few seconds I saw quite a large black shiny snake curled up on the ground, like a glossy inner tube and I was just about to stand on it! I froze with fright then stepped sideways as we went back into darkness. I was absolutely petrified, but luckily another vehicle's beams a few seconds later lit up the area and the snake had slithered God knows where! Thank goodness it happened to be our hotel bus returning so we quickly flagged it down and climbed aboard, thinking how fortunate I had been.

Although only seen briefly, I was able to describe the snake to the driver and he said it was more than likely to be one of the deadliest snakes in Thailand ...a black cobra and if bitten, one has only about thirty minutes to be administered a serum. After that traumatic event we decided to stay in our hotel bar that evening and count our blessings. That certainly was a narrow escape! The next morning around the town there were many very small dead snakes washed up through the drains, smaller versions of the cobra perhaps?

At the end of each evening into the early hours, it was delightful to just sit on our balcony with a drink or three, listening to the sound of hundreds of crickets and occasional frogs croaking in with their background vocals. We would sometimes, out of the corner of our eyes, see small green geckos racing up the walls then suddenly come to a full stop. The next morning they would still be there in the exact same place, completely motionless as though they were made out of clay. They were such cute little creatures so we bought a large replica of one which has sat on the bathroom window ledge ever since.

At this time, I did have a mobile phone but because of the poor reception, I chose to 'phone home' by using a special card to slot into the public phone situated on the beach. As soon as I connected with my father, he anxiously said it must be costing me a fortune ringing from so far away, so he would not talk for very long! He failed to acknowledge the amazing fact that I was standing on a beach thousands of miles away having a conversation in roasting hot temperatures while he was freezing in England. I think he was secretly pleased, though, that I was taking time out to chat to him whatever the cost, which was actually only about five pounds each time.

Koh Samui Night Life

'A company of lady boys put on
a spectacular performance'

During our time there, we grew to love Koh Samui more every day and planned to return in the future, as we became acquainted with the Jah Dub beach bar and the Reggae Pub (only opened in 1989), which was then the main night club. To reach the latter, which was situated alongside a lake, we had to pass through an area which was more or less a 'red light' district. The girls were over-friendly of course, but not threatening in any way, so we ran the gauntlet without any bother. The main DJ there was a guy called Sergio who had emigrated from Palermo, Italy. Aside from him playing major dance tracks, many live bands also appeared, but a highlight on a Sunday was the 'Singha Gold Beer Drinking' contest. Contestants had to drink 4 bottles each and the fastest consumers won the T Shirts featuring the Club's logo. Had we taken part we would probably have both been sick so we never attempted it!

Nearby was a very chilled out place called 'The Club' which played mostly laid-back easy listening lounge music tinged with jazz, so it was nice to just relax there occasionally. One cluster of bars in Chaweng, which was not to our tastes at all, was called the Green Mango Resort! Every bar belted out dance music louder than the one next door and what a cacophony of noise it was. I can remember Cher's 'Believe' battling with Madonna's 'Frozen' and it was difficult to decide who was the winner! Bars called the Black Jack Pub, Fawlty Towers, Charlie's Pub and Di's Place will give you a flavour of what to expect! (Bars with similar names were also popular in Magaluf, Mallorca when mistakenly we went on holiday there to our regret!) One visit to the GM was enough so we avoided it from then on, but on this occasion though, we did succeed in having a side-splitting moment.

A very large lady full of the joys of alcohol, was dancing happily back and forward till she fell backwards into a terracotta plant pot and became firmly wedged in it. Her friends had to tip her over onto her front till she looked like a giant turtle, to enable them to prise her out of it. The whole bar was laughing hysterically including her and us too! We did actually return to that area once more on a later holiday in 2004. We had met a crowd of young Australians staying in our hotel and we had several nights out with them, mainly for meals. They persuaded us to go to the Green Mango with them one night so we half-heartedly agreed. Tequila shots were being passed around with various other concoctions in 'fish bowls' and we thoroughly enjoyed what we remember about it! I know we had to get a taxi back to the hotel and didn't surface till lunchtime the following day, nursing very bad heads. Our friends thought we were really cool after that, considering we were nearly twice their ages! We decided not to repeat the experience though!

Another favourite beach haunt of ours was the Ark Bar. They played mostly dance music but as the evening progressed, the ambience became more subdued. Tracks like Chris Rea's 'On The Beach', Dido's 'Here With Me' and George Michael's 'Careless Whisper' slotted into the chilled out atmosphere perfectly. It was also possible to stay in some basic studio accommodation amongst the palm trees behind the bar, but it was mainly designed for students and backpackers. Cheap and cheerful it was, but not for us though, as we preferred something a bit more luxurious!

In central Chaweng on the main street, were a number of bars where a company of 'lady boys' performed spectacular shows as though they were headlining in Las Vegas. Unfortunately, their attempts were spoiled a little by their inability to lip synch successfully to songs like 'Ain't No Mountain High Enough', 'Big Spender' and 'I Wanna Be Loved By You'. They simply did not understand what the words meant and what they were supposed to be miming to! Three of them did a fabulous version of the Ronettes 'Be My Baby' in tight skirts and huge beehive wigs! The result was hilarious and highly entertaining! I have to admit though, that these 'lady boys' excelled in looking convincingly like the glamorous women they portrayed, such as Diana Ross, Shirley Bassey and Marilyn Monroe. That illusion was quickly dispelled when one of them kissed me on the cheek and I realised that Miss Bassey had forgotten to shave that evening!

Behind Chaweng's main street close to the Star Gym, we could walk through to Laemdin Market to a food court full of stalls selling street food. Whatever you chose could be eaten at any table and the atmosphere was so magical but quite humid at 2am. After all the spicy dishes, we would round it off with banana pancakes cooked on a roadside stall. There were also ice cream parlours situated here and there selling a vast array of exotic flavours we had never tasted before, in England at least. We spent many happy times in those too.

On that first holiday, we spent most early evenings on the beach around 5pm sampling different cocktails. One night, as the garlands of lights began to light up the palm trees, we were both sprawled in our deckchairs, sipping our 'zombies' in absolute bliss. Suddenly my mobile phone started ringing. Thinking it might be my father, I answered it and discovered it was Macclesfield Borough Council! "We are just bringing your attention to your unpaid council tax Mr Cooper". I didn't dare mention that we were in Thailand on an exotic holiday and hoped they couldn't hear the sound of a steel band in the background! I told them we had to unexpectedly go to a family funeral in London and we had overlooked the payment. We agreed to settle it as soon as we returned home. That put a slight damper on our enjoyment for the moment, but it did make us laugh, especially as we wondered who the dear departed was supposed to be! I don't know how much the call cost MBC! Always get your priorities right, I say! They got paid in due course and we had a fabulous holiday. A win-win situation!

In writing this book, it would be so easy to go down the expected route of covering every single aspect of Samui life as portrayed in a tourist guide. The attractions are limitless but we are telling our story based on what we actually did. Naturally, we visited many of the recommended sights, so can relate the experiences we had in those places. If we did not go there, we have not written about it. We could also have visited the snake and crocodile farms, but after our brush with that cobra, we decided it was not so appealing! We did take a short ride on an elephant, which was slightly scary wobbling from side to side, as we approached a huge spider dangling from a palm leaf. As we were brushing past it, I managed to duck far enough out of the way to avoid it dropping on my head. I would have launched myself off that elephant like an Exocet missile, make no mistake!

Getting round the island was particularly easy, firstly in 'songthaews' which were red converted pickup trucks containing two long bench seats facing each other. They covered most destinations for a reasonable cost, but prices increased in the evening. Alternatively, there were yellow air-conditioned taxis which were quicker and obviously more expensive. One experience in a songthaew was hilarious as we had a goat on board as well as a cage full of chickens! Passengers sat on the roof and also hung off the back like it was perfectly normal. I cannot envisage that on the Bollington bus to Macclesfield!

On this holiday, we were fortunate to use the services of a member of our hotel staff at the Novotel Mercure as a guide on his day off. His name was Pong, but I am pleased to say he did not live up to the name! He drove us to a selection of important places around the island, like the Butterfly Farm in the south, which was amazingly beautiful. Some of the butterflies were housed in a conservatory style building but they were also freely flying through all the exotic foliage outside which was encased in netting. The keeper usually placed their favourite food like sweet bananas and bright red hibiscus flowers at different points along the walkways. These were the best places to stand and watch the multicoloured specimens in closeup and take any photos. There was also a museum displaying dried preserved versions of these creatures, after they had passed on.

We were also taken to the Monkey Theatre to watch various species performing on stage, riding bicycles and climbing up palm trees collecting coconuts. They sometimes mischievously threw them down at the watching crowd, so you had to make sure you knew when to duck! The latter job was perfectly natural to them, but neither of us really agreed with making animals perform human feats. It was amusing, but it did make us wonder how intensely the monkeys were coerced to achieve their cycling skills. This venue was situated at the entrance to Kow Pra village near Bophut should anyone wish to visit, but make sure you take a crash helmet!

This beautiful island had now well and truly gotten under our skins and we decided that it would not be the last time we holidayed there. The particularly long journey was a small price to pay to enjoy such a scenic and memorable country, so we decided that we would more than likely return there the following year. So with that in our minds, we flew back to England unaware that our next holiday would dramatically change our lives forever!

Return To Koh Samui

'We tried hard to stifle our amusement by hiding behind large slices of watermelon'

Welcome to Koh Samui. Do you like doggies? If you do you are lucky, as they are all over the island. You will find them at the beach, outside restaurants and around swimming pools. There are around 5000 of these cute canine creatures and nobody really cares for them except the Dog Rescue Centre.

(Samui Welcome Newspaper, Jan 1999)

In 1999 after much thought, we decided to spend our second holiday there in February, this time for three weeks and once again took it upon ourselves to feed the dogs whenever we could. In the space of twelve months, Chaweng had now concreted the coastal road that ran through the town and had built several more modernised shops and restaurants, including a second supermarket.

The Dog Rescue Centre Samui (DRCS) had also just begun their invaluable work of caring for injured and sick dogs free of charge, relying on donations from tourists, local people and even some of the hotels. 'Samui Welcome' was a local newspaper written in English, German and Thai, and it was from that we first became aware of the work the DRCS was doing. They were also taking dogs from the beach and vaccinating, spaying and castrating them in order to help reduce the dog population.

On this visit, our choice of hotel was the Baan Samui Hotel at the opposite end to the DRCS, and on the beach near the hotel we began to regularly feed a number of dogs. One afternoon outside the Hotel Samui Natien, which was a few hundred yards further along, one of these dogs very similar to a labrador, all black with four white paws was still lying contentedly on the sand next to us. It was apparent that she had quite recently given birth to a litter of pups. We had seen her the previous day there too, so we decided we should give her a name, as we suspected our paths would cross quite often. As she spent her time wandering along different stretches of beach, we decided on the name of Gypsy. We wondered how she had kept herself in such good condition, but apart from a few small white scars on her legs and stomach and a rather spindly tail, she had a glossy coat and was lean without being scrawny.

We packed up our towels and sun lotion and wondered what we were now going to do with this dog that had faithfully kept us company for the past few hours. We decided to take her to the supermarket to buy a tin of dog meat and a bottle of water. Whilst standing outside waiting for Phil to come back, I was horrified to see a small panting dog frantically running past me, and on his back was a gaping hole with a bleeding muscle clearly visible. It had probably been involved in a dog fight or hit by a car, but within seconds it had vanished. It must have been in excruciating agony. I told Phil as soon as he returned and we rushed in the direction the dog had gone, hoping to find it but to no avail. We felt totally powerless and that vision stayed in my mind for a long time afterwards.

After I had calmed down from that incredibly upsetting sight, we tipped the tin of dog meat onto a piece of cardboard and Phil filled his beach cap up with cold water. After Gypsy's appetite was satisfied, we took her through the town back to the beach. She at first stood watching us as we started to head in the direction of our hotel and slowly and hesitantly began to follow us. We already knew she would not be welcome in the hotel, so we did not encourage her. On reaching our hotel, we observed members of staff busy laying tables for dinner and wondered if they would notice us with a dog trailing behind us. She continued to trot proudly beside us till we reached the steps leading up to our room, then came to a halt. We carried on without looking back. A few minutes later we heard a scratching at the door and whimpering. When we opened it, there was Gypsy staring at us. She waited until we beckoned her in and she let out a long drawn out sound, like a cow mooing only more high pitched. This we came to know as her way of saying 'I like this'! She immediately settled herself down near the air-conditioning vents, which was absolute luxury for a dog constantly living in temperatures of around 33 degrees centigrade day and night. She also discovered there was a plentiful supply of water in the toilet bowl!

For several consecutive nights this happened, and we were able to leave her there for two or three hours each night while we went out for a meal and drinks. She would stay the night, sleeping in close proximity to the cool circulating air, until we let her out very early in the morning before the hotel staff were about. Every time we returned, she excitedly wagged her tail when we gave her something we had brought back from our meals.

Thinking and hoping that someone may have taken the injured dog I saw outside the supermarket to the clinic, we decided to pay them a visit the following morning.

Unfortunately, they knew nothing about it, so it worried us even more. The morning we were there, someone had just anonymously left a small cage containing four puppies outside the building in a cardboard box. As they were so hungry, three of them had started gnawing on the other pup's legs, so they were immediately separated. The vet carefully cleaned the wounds and gave it antibiotics, and I believe it did survive along with the rest of the litter. I am not sure whether homes were found for any of them though. I am hoping so.

We saw a few other tragic sights in there which are difficult to comment on, but one dog had a tumour on one leg the size of a grapefruit. Another had lost both back legs because of a car accident and dragged itself along the ground by its front legs. In a matter of days, though, she was attached to a contraption with wheels, so that was much easier for the dog. Despite their afflictions, it amazed us how unconcerned they seemed, always wagging their tails when we talked to them.

While we were there, we gave a donation and started to get to know more about Brigitte and Werner. They were more or less based there for most of the year and just returned to Berlin over the Christmas period. They both had quite elderly parents to visit, but Werner also went home for two weeks in summer to produce their annual accounts. While they were away, volunteers like ourselves usually took charge at the centre.

I must mention that on arrival at our hotel, we were given literature that included the following words of advice:

> *Be aware! Please do not feed the dogs on the beach, as it encourages more, and they become a serious risk and possible danger to children. We ask you to ignore the dogs, and they will go away. Note that dogs are not allowed on the hotel premises either. Thank you.*

Well, we had already broken that rule but thought that if we were careful, it would go unnoticed, and so far, so good. We realised gradually that a couple staying opposite our apartment always stared intently at us, particularly when they saw us with Gypsy and muttered under their breaths. They glared at us over their abundant supply of cocktails, and we got the impression they were definitely not dog lovers!

On the evenings we spent socialising with friends from the hotel, we usually sat on benches or deck chairs round wooden tables, just a matter of feet from the waves whispering onto the shoreline. It was usually outside the Jah Dub, which was adjacent to our hotel. One night, about 2 am, we heard some loud giggling sounds coming from the beach in front of the Baan Samui. In the twilight we could see a group of several people placing towels on the beach beds, ready for the morning. I have to mention that they were from Germany; now how unexpected was that? Phil stared at me with a grin on his face and said, "I know what we're going to do," and laughed. I was immediately on the same wavelength.

After it had gone quiet, we decided to 'rearrange' all the towels to be as confusing as possible, even hiding a couple up a palm tree. There were at least a dozen. We came down to breakfast early next morning and sat there waiting to witness the outcome. It was so hilarious, but we tried hard to stifle our amusement by hiding behind large slices of watermelon. I do not know any swear words in German, but I am sure someone must have said something like, 'Who the bloody hell's done this?' or worse! Action taken; result achieved! We think it may have made them think twice about doing it again.

Whilst in the hotel, we became friends with a young couple from Rochdale called Barbara and Steve. She worked for the estate agents, Bradford and Bingley, and he was a security guard for V.I.P. people, but he gave us no indication as to who they were. All very hush-hush! The more we got to know them, we found them to be so set in their ways, or at least Barbara was. Every day after breakfast, Barbara sat in the same deck chair by the pool, immersed in a book. I think she must have waded through at least four while Steve sunbathed and occasionally swam in the pool or the sea with us.

As the holiday progressed, he spent more and more time in our company, chatting and enjoying drinks on our balcony. Frustratingly for us, they never joined us for an evening meal anywhere else but the one restaurant they went to every night. This was called the Riverside, situated on the opposite side of the road our hotel was on. With so many different places to choose from, we found it so difficult to persuade them to try somewhere new with us. On their last night they finally relented and joined us, and we spent a lovely evening at the Magic Light. The restaurant was Swiss owned, so the menu was a combination of Swiss and Thai dishes. During the holiday the couple never explored the island or booked any excursions, until I managed to persuade Steve to join us one day on a snorkelling trip to Ko Tao, a nearby island. Barbara reluctantly decided to accompany us, and they actually admitted afterwards that it was the best day they had all holiday! Talk about missed opportunities!

The following day was their final day, or they would have ventured further afield, I think. We felt decidedly sorry for Steve because we could tell he was held back by his wife's lack of enthusiasm. We kept in touch with them for over two years, after which Steve wrote and told us that they had mutually decided to go their separate ways. He was planning to return to the island again with his two best friends, but we refrained from mentioning that we could see that breakup coming. It was a shame, as we loved them both equally.

On one day when we didn't see Gypsy, we decided to go swimming at a famous waterfall called Na Muang 1, which is about 20 metres high. Walking along the path towards it, on the left we became aware of a huge spider's web at least eight foot across suspended between the fronds of two palm trees. The web strands appeared to be made of thick rope! I dread to think of how large the spider would have been to have created this, and thankfully it was not currently in residence. Further on, rocks and tree roots formed a natural staircase leading directly to a large pool at the base of the waterfall. We confidently swam there, knowing it was unlikely that this giant arachnid would be doing the breaststroke beside us as the water cascaded around us. On our way back we observed that the web was still minus its occupant! We did wonder where it was lurking, though! Just the mere sight of it would have put me on a stretcher!

Heartbreak Hotel!

'The dog situation on the island does not worry me in the slightest, sir.'

Next morning, we woke up and were shocked to find an envelope pushed under our door. Inside was a letter from the hotel manager regarding Gypsy staying in our room. Apparently, some hotel guests, more than likely the ones we suspected, had reported seeing Gypsy climbing up the stairs on the way to our room the evening before.

Dear Sir,

I wish to inform you that it is against hotel policy to keep dogs in your room. We are sorry but we do not encourage or allow the dogs to enter the hotel grounds, as the next guest coming maybe does not like dogs and we receive many complaints every year about them. Please consider another person.

Guest Relations.

We were very disappointed but agreed to abide by their wishes to avoid being asked to leave the hotel or pay additional charges. Thankfully, it appeared that the informants had now gone home, so we broke the rules several times more and risked sneaking her in, but then received a second, more detailed letter.

Dear Sir,

This is the second letter I am forced to write to you regarding the dogs. It is not hotel policy to allow the dogs into the hotel grounds and especially not in the rooms. It is unhygienic and it is unfair to the next guests who occupy your room. It also causes additional work for the housekeeping department. Therefore I regret to inform you, we will be charging you 500 baht for damage to the bed sheets, i.e. dog hair which is difficult to remove and we will continue to charge you if the dog continues to visit your room.

Guest Relations

Well, for a few days we restrained ourselves from letting Gypsy in, but it was considerably difficult, as you can imagine. We received a third letter as follows...more or less a repeat of the earlier letter.

> *Dear Sirs,*
>
> *Another complaint has been made that you are keeping a dog in your room. This is NOT hotel policy as it is unfair to the next guests that occupy it and it also causes additional work for the housekeeping department. Therefore we will be adding 500 Thai baht per day to your bill for the damage to the bed cover as dog hair is difficult to remove. We will continue to charge you this amount as long as the animal visits your room.*
>
> *Guest Relations.*

We were getting very exasperated by all these notes, so I told Phil I would liaise with the young lady in Guest Relations who was from England. I told her that it was only the tourists who showed the dogs any love and affection and made sure there was food available for them. I explained that we were being very careful keeping the room free of dog hair, but it made no difference. Her attitude was unbelievably harsh! "The dog situation on the island does not worry me in the slightest, sir. Making sure the guests have a good holiday is all I am interested in, and most of them don't like dogs. I've got to do what I'm paid for. We receive complaint after complaint about them. My duty is to the holidaymakers, not the dogs, who will always find some way of surviving...they always do."

"I guessed as much, and I am so shocked about the way you feel! I have never met anyone so heartless!" I replied and walked off. Not a caring bone in her body with a heart of stone was the opinion I came away with. I suppose it was more important to her to keep her job, so I saw where she was coming from in that way, sadly.

Considering their attitude over keeping dogs in the hotel, they were totally unconcerned about something that bothered us. Our next-door neighbours constantly argued, virtually every night, mostly in the early hours, mostly after heavy drinking sessions. I banged hard on the wall one night, and all they did was knock back twice as loud! The staff in reception said that it was none of their business and if it annoyed us, we should go round and chat to them about it!! We then asked to be moved to another room, but before that happened, the couple checked out separately, which did not surprise us at all!

We decided we would have to ignore Gypsy each time she started scratching the door in the early hours. After a few minutes she would give up and we would watch her below us from our balcony, trotting through the hotel grounds with her tail down. Inevitably, we gave in yet again and risked it near the end of our holiday. Half an hour after sneaking her out at 6:30am, there was a loud knock on the door. "I wonder who that can be Bob?" said Phil, grinning from ear to ear. Of course, it was the manager this time in person saying he had just witnessed Gypsy going down the steps on her way back to the beach, so we could not deny it. We apologised profusely and said we will be going back to England soon and we promise that it will definitely be the last time she stays. We told Mr. Songkrasin that we were being considerate by buying a roll of Sellotape and using it to remove any dog hairs we noticed from the bedding and floor, but he just scowled.

During the daytime, each morning Gypsy would usually be waiting on the beach for us, and on days when we were a little late, she would venture part of the way into the pool area to see if we were there. Fortunately, the bar staff were quite tolerant of her lying with us near the swimming pool, so quite often we were able to do that, well out of sight of reception. Gypsy always enjoyed running into the sea with us, cooling herself down from the intense heat, and one day she ended up floating beside me on my water bed. This caused great amusement amongst the holidaymakers sunbathing on the beach and swimming close by. They could not believe their eyes, and this was captured on cameras by a few onlookers. She definitely enjoyed those unusual and luxurious moments, as did we.

Because of the constant traffic along the main road, we decided to buy a collar and dog lead and train Gypsy to walk alongside us. This meant we could go into the town without fear of her running off and being hit by a car, which was a regular occurrence with so many dogs on the loose. On the beach we always removed the lead so she could run freely whenever she wanted, but she always came back to us. We also taught her to give us her paw in exchange for a biscuit, bearing in mind that it was a way of her asking for food from new people she might meet, after we'd gone home. Whilst wearing a collar, she was also less likely to be targeted for poisoning as it would have been presumed she was owned by someone. I inscribed her name on the collar in indelible ink in large letters.

Before we were due to leave for England, we decided to take Gypsy and another dog we named Francis to be vaccinated against rabies. At least we could go home knowing that they would not be stricken by this horrific disease, although on Koh Samui at that time, there had been no rabies cases for eight years, so was virtually eradicated.

When our last evening arrived, we decided to choose a popular restaurant on the beach, near the water's edge.

We had dined there once before and It was beautifully lit up with strings of lights and lanterns dangling from the palm trees fringing the shore. Gypsy was with us too and she settled down after digging a hole in the sand and went to sleep under our table. We ordered our meals and a bottle of Mekong, which we had become very partial to. It was so relaxing listening to the waves rolling over the sand, until suddenly the manager appeared wielding a long broom. I thought wrongly that he was kindly going to smooth out the sand around us. Far from it as he proceeded to prod Gypsy vigorously with it. This resulted in a huge argument as we tried to prevent him from hitting her, so I said to Phil 'Come on let's go! We're not eating here now'.

Because I was so angry, I could not resist smashing my plate of sweet and sour shark onto the table and every diner received a free sample! I remembered to snatch our bottle of drink off the table before we started to run with Gypsy along Chaweng beach. This man was like a whirling dervish, flinging his spinning broom across the sand apparently attempting to catch Gypsy's ankles, but instead caught the back of one of Phil's. After a brief wrestling match I managed to wrench the broom out of his grasp and flung it as far as I could into the sea. If I could have lifted him up too, he would have ended up going in the same direction! Satisfied that he had done some damage, the restaurant owner ran back to his establishment. Unfortunately he had managed to snatch Phil's shoulder bag off him, which contained our passports, Thai baht and other important items so I was soon hot on his heels back into the restaurant.

After a very heated exchange I agreed to pay him for the main course they had brought to the table plus the broken plate and the bottle of Mekong, because he was threatening to call the police. I informed him that we had plenty of witnesses regarding his cruel behaviour and that would be reported to them. To be truthful, he probably did not understand most of what I was saying. Not wanting the situation to escalate further as it was becoming so stressful we just wanted to be out of this scenario. I descended the wooden steps from the restaurant onto the sand and suddenly became aware of a huge audience of diners watching me incredulously!

In a few second flashback I remembered a scene in a Bette Davis film called 'The Anniversary'. She was descending a long flight of stairs wearing a patch over one eye and announced as only she could to her family "So you found my glass eye?" This was said to her grandson who had taken his girlfriend into her bedroom. In this very same vein I could not resist remarking loudly (minus eye patch), 'I bet THAT'S been a nice evening's entertainment for you, hasn't it?' No one uttered a word. They would not forget that night out in a hurry and nor would we! A few of them actually applauded, obviously being dog lovers. I just smiled at them but refrained from actually bowing though it was very tempting! I missed out on receiving an Oscar that night, I think!

I ran after Phil, who was limping along the beach till we reached the Jah Dub beach bar we'd visited so many times before and spent what was left of our last evening there, where Gypsy was always welcome. (When we returned home, Phil had to attend a gruelling course of physiotherapy for six weeks). We sneaked Gypsy into our room again that night as we were going home the next day and quite honestly did not give a damn anyway. We let her out at 6am, as we had done on many previous occasions. There were no repercussions this time, but we would not have cared if there had been. What an awful ending to the final night of our holiday, though!

The following morning after breakfast, a violent storm struck the resort with torrential rain gradually flooding the roads and pavements. There was no sign of Gypsy on the beach, which worried us in case she had disappeared for the day. What problems that would have caused. We borrowed umbrellas and wandered along the sand past places we had previously been with her and eventually encountered her creeping out of a beach hut. Obviously, she had sought shelter when the storm began. We both had a sinking feeling in our stomachs when it dawned on us that this would be the last day we would all be on this beach together. We knew all too well what was due to happen, but Gypsy was totally oblivious to this forthcoming separation.

We were dreading the time when we would have to leave for the airport, knowing we would most likely never see our beautiful four-legged friend again. She stayed with us the whole day, going everywhere we went, to the bank, the souvenir shops, the cafes and the bars, and for a last swim. We packed so much into the last day of the holiday and wished it could have lasted forever. We could not even imagine how we were going to cope when it came to actually leaving Gypsy behind and what would be the effect on her.

At around 4pm we had to return to our hotel to collect our luggage and begin our epic journey back home to England. This was such an ordeal as we piled our cases alongside the others by the hotel minibus. We knelt down and hugged Gypsy with tears in our eyes and said our goodbyes. She looked very bewildered as we climbed into the vehicle and sat next to some other guests also leaving for home. One friend we had made said, "We've watched you throughout the holiday become so close to that dog. You must be heartbroken." I was too choked up to answer and just tearfully nodded.

As we pulled away, Gypsy started howling, frantically running from side to side. As our bus drew further away from the hotel, we could see her still watching us, seemingly very confused as to where to go next. It was the most awful experience we had ever had as we saw her dwindle to a speck in the distance. Phil looked at me and in a wavering voice said, "She'll be alright, Bob! She will find someone else like us to look after her!" Sounding quite unconvincing, those words were of no consolation, and I knew deep down he was as worried and upset as I was. We could not begin to think what was going on in Gypsy's mind. Does a dog ever wonder why someone they love just goes out of their life forever? Had she gone through traumatic moments like this before? It just didn't bear thinking about as the minibus put an ever-stretching distance between us.

When we reached the airport, we could barely speak as we went through the motions of checking our luggage in. As we ascended the plane steps, we knew that once we had boarded, that would be it, and there was no going back. As our plane rose into the night sky heading for Bangkok, we could see below us rows of twinkling lights along Chaweng beach. We knew that somewhere down there, Gypsy was either curled up in the sand near our hotel or wandering along the beach searching for something to eat. We hoped and prayed that someone else would befriend her like we did and feed her while they were there. It was an extremely sad and emotional journey home with the memories that were entrenched in our hearts and minds.

As depressed as we were on arriving home, when we switched on the BBC TV news, we were devastated to see scenes from Dusty Springfield's funeral! We were unaware she had passed away but did know she was having treatment for cancer for the second time. Always on holiday, we used to extricate ourselves from the world and never read any newspapers or watch television. We were in a world free from the media, so you can imagine the shock when learning that a singer whose career I had followed since her Springfields days and had met a few times had left us at the young age of 59, far too soon. To this day she has attained a legendary status and is more appreciated than ever.

Third Time Lucky?

'Do you always lie under a grilling machine before you come to Koh Samui?'

Since leaving Gypsy on the beautiful Koh Samui, over one year had passed, but for the third time we were heading back there full of mixed emotions. Never had a day gone by since our last holiday where she did not enter our thoughts. Naturally, we hoped that Gypsy would be there waiting for us, but on the other hand, if we were unable to find her, it would indeed have been soul-destroying. So much time had gone by that we wondered if she would remember us or even worse, would she still be alive?

At that time, some cruel hotel owners deliberately fed the feral dogs poisoned meat in order to deplete the dog population, particularly the ones that gathered near their hotels. At the time of writing this is only a very minor occurrence, thanks to the work done by the DRCS. Gradually, they have considerably whittled down these incidents and they always report any establishment still doing this to the Thai Government. They also have a 'black list' of 'non-dog-friendly hotels' which visiting dog lovers can view and therefore avoid booking them. This alone has made the majority of these erring hotels cease this cruel practice. Many of these establishments have also been persuaded to place donation boxes in their reception areas along with information leaflets. Uppermost in our minds as we approached our destination was the worry that something tragic could have happened to Gypsy since our last time on the island.

As we had enjoyed it so much, we had decided to book the Baan Samui Hotel again, where we had stayed the previous year, just in case 'our dog' was still in that vicinity. This was despite the negative attitude and confrontations we had had with the hotel management. On arrival there, the reception staff seemed considerably amused and we soon realised why! Some of them we were familiar with from the previous year and they had booked us into a room only accessible by passing through the reception area! Remembering our last holiday there, the hotel manager was obviously determined to prevent us bringing any dogs into their hotel on this occasion! Very calculating by them and considerably frustrating to us!

After settling in, our first thought was to head for the beach and see if our hopes would be realised, but of course, straight away they were dashed as Gypsy was nowhere to be seen. We came to the conclusion that we were being highly optimistic, expecting a situation thousands of miles away to still be exactly the same as when we had left it, thirteen months earlier. The first five days of our holiday were spent chilling out and enjoying the sun, sea and sand, but at the same time we were keeping our eyes open for this one dog that had affected our lives so much the year before.

One disappointing observation we made was that many of the small beach bar shacks we had been visiting the previous year had disappeared, like 'Cheers', 'Bamboo' and 'Coconut Bay' to name just three. The former used to play every night, the Verve's 'Bitter Sweet Symphony', so whenever we have heard that song since, it immediately transports us back to those magical balmy nights under the stars with various friends the year before. Apparently, the reason why those bars were vanishing was that travel companies were buying up the space to build their sumptuous all-inclusive hotels. Unfortunately, this is what growing popularity causes when visiting exotic holiday destinations and it eventually ruins somewhere that used to be very rustic and unspoilt. It also takes away the natural way of life that locals operate with their small businesses. If they were employed by the hotels, their wages were very basic and caused much poverty. A TV documentary produced by Stacey Dooley on BBC2 featured this aspect recently.

On this holiday, we made friends with a family that lived in County Down, Ireland. Their favourite drinking holes were the Samui Shamrock and the Moby Dick Irish bars so we felt obliged to go there with them a couple of times. It was strange seeing bottles of Guinness on the shelves next to Chang beer! Of course, they had to feature ceilidh bands to create the Irish atmosphere but we resisted doing something from Michael Flatley's 'Riverdance'!

For anyone that enjoys snorkelling, which we did, virtually every beach is perfect for that, but we also chose to take excursions to other islands close by. Before boarding the boats, we were all issued with flippers, life jackets and snorkelling equipment in the Bophut dive shop. One such trip was to Ko Tao and it was absolute bliss swimming through shoals of the most colourful fish imaginable of all shapes and sizes, like angel, butterfly and parrot fish to name just a few. Regrettably, we experienced an incident which really made us both livid.

In one of the bays we visited, we witnessed a party of young Japanese tourists bouncing up and down in the water with open plastic bags. They were attempting to scoop the fish into them! What on earth they were going to do with them when they returned to their hotels I cannot imagine. Between us, we tried to thwart this awful act of vandalism as much as possible by swimming very inconveniently between them and the fish! One young guy caught three angel fish in his bag and tied a knot in it. I made him undo it and empty them back into the sea and took this opportunity to loudly say, "You know this is completely wrong, so why are you doing it?" and I think he understood me. Well, it seemed to work as they all left the water and sat huddled together on the beach, glaring daggers at us! No doubt they probably returned to the scene of the crime after we had moved on, though.

There are of course many different water sports to enjoy, like kayaking, jet skiing, wind surfing, and paragliding. These were mostly off limits for me as, being a cameraman full time, I was afraid of injuring myself, which would have prevented me filming all my bookings. There was also the possibility of causing damage to my camera. One occasion that suddenly made me aware of this was when we were climbing up a sheer rockface on tiny, jagged steps to reach a view of a lagoon, with my left hand holding my camera. One slip and that would have been it for me and the camera, so I became very sensible from that moment on! I was not averse to snorkelling though, when I would not have had my camera with me!

On a musical note, we used to travel around the island through avenues of palm trees in Brigitte's car on the way to Ban Taling Ngam where the recently opened rescue centre was. She used to play us a cassette of the singer Edgar Murray, a popular entertainer from Germany who lived there. His most famous song was the highly originally titled 'Koh Samui'. This was a very lilting and rhythmic reggae song extolling the virtues of visiting the island and was popular everywhere. He was an important asset to the DRCS as he performed in cabaret at places like Montien House on Chaweng beach to help raise funds.

Another singer was Ritchie Newman also from Berlin, who was among other things, an Elvis impersonator. He did a specific concert as Elvis in a night club when we were there and this helped to boost the donations. He also appeared several times a week at the Samui Natien Hotel. You have probably gathered by now that Reggae had a considerable influence on the music scene by the naming of the Jah Dub and Reggae Pub. Bob Marley was played everywhere even though Thailand was thousands of miles from the Caribbean. At the entrance to the Jah Dub there was a huge poster of the great legend hanging from the wall.

When we first visited to Koh Samui, many of the stall holders round Chaweng markets sold trays full of audio cassettes of all the latest albums for around 50p each! They were obviously bootlegs, which was very apparent by the amateurish packaging. We must admit to buying many of those. Even DVDs were on sale for a £1 and the quality was questionable, but we also took advantage of the very low prices. We bought the Mel Gibson film, 'The Passion of the Christ' and when watching it back home, we were surprised to see these shadowy figures going past in different scenes every so often. It suddenly dawned on us that someone must have re-filmed this from the big screen from the back of a cinema and then transferred it onto a DVD! The shadows were members of the audience! The lengths people will go to to make some money! Next it was unofficial CDs being reproduced and presented in a more professional quality, so how they surmounted copyright laws I will never know! They probably just turned a blind eye to them until they were found out, if they ever were.

Brigitte's command of English was phenomenal, but on occasions her choice of words was not always appropriate, though we always knew what she meant. We laughed when she asked us on one holiday "Do you always lie under a grilling machine before you come to Koh Samui?" We pointed out that we call them sunbeds in England! Likewise with her husband Werner, he occasionally trotted out a comment which made us smile.

We went to meet him at Montien House Beach Hotel one evening and asked him where Brigitte was. "My wife, she is so deranged!" he remarked. I asked him why. "The electricity went off when she was washing her hair and she has not been able to use her computer either! She will be very late!" I think he could have chosen the phrase. 'she is in a rage' or perhaps 'annoyed' to be more precise, rather than give the impression she was mentally unstable! She turned up eventually with one of the rescue dogs Blindy (rhymes with windy).This lovely happy dog was born without any eyes, yet despite this serious disability, he was continually wagging his tale and scampering around like any normal dog.

While Brigitte and Werner were waiting for their bungalow to be built behind Laemdin Market in the centre of Chaweng, by the owner of Montien House, they stayed at the hotel for a couple of months. Ten dogs also lived in the grounds with their own kennels, which was a very kind gesture. Once their bungalow was completed, it also became the home for approximately thirty dogs and fifteen cats. Amazingly, they co-existed quite well apart from the occasional spats! The situation eased once the animal shelter was opened and eventually the cats had their own section with about 70 living permanently there. There were also 44 cages for the dogs undergoing treatment and twelve large enclosures for them to exercise and live in.

The Songkran Festival

'Despite their protests they ended up
like drowned rats within seconds!'

On this particular holiday, we had chosen to go back there in April, to tie in with the Songkran festival, which is on the 13th and 14th every year. It is to celebrate the Thai New Year and water is the central element in this festival. Buddha images, both public and private are washed in lustral water...for a clean start. Then the public are cleansed by being hosed down by all members of the community whether one likes it or not! Being a video cameraman, I obviously wanted to capture as much of this special event as possible, so I decided to start filming it outside our hotel. Suddenly a truck pulled up, and five young Thai guys leapt onto the pavement carrying buckets of water. They immediately headed towards us with the obvious intention of soaking us to the skin! I was of course worried that my camera would have been saturated and more than likely ruined, so I confronted the first man and pointed at my camera and shouted "Don't you DARE!" By the mischievous look on his face, it seemed to me he was still determined to do it, so I turned my back on him and quickly handed the camera to the barman, who placed it on a high shelf.

    I was so disappointed about not being able to film this unusual occurrence, but had to ensure my camera was safe. We were then easy targets, so had to suffer being drenched for the second time that day. We had only just dried out from our early morning attack! Anticipating a possible third soaking, we decided that evening to walk a considerable way along the beach to the highly recommended Poppies Hotel and restaurant. We chose a table on the sand and am glad to say we remained dry for the duration of our three-course meal and drinks.

    We left the restaurant via the main entrance, hoping we would not be attacked again by the locals wielding water containers! A young couple was standing on the steps dressed very elegantly, particularly the woman. She wore a long slim silvery evening dress and reminded me of a young Joan Collins. They were waiting for a taxi, but instead a tuk-tuk suddenly appeared and three guys scrambled out with the inevitable buckets full of cold water. Despite their protests they ended up like drowned rats within seconds! 'Joan' burst into tears but her man friend was trying very hard to stifle a grin, as he could see us both also trying to hold back our laughter. "I told you we should have dressed down tonight after what happened earlier! Now what?" he muttered to her. "We're going back to our room and won't be coming out again." she sobbed.

Watching all this meant we were caught off guard, then all of a sudden it was our turn again and we squelched back to our hotel along the water's edge after our final soaking of the day! To be honest, it did not bother us at all as we were only wearing T shirts and shorts and we were getting accustomed to it anyway. And it cooled us down too! All part of the fun and the culture. It is a very sensible idea to read up in advance about a country's traditions and if something is likely to upset you, just choose another time to visit. Or travel to another destination.

In between all these events we were enjoying, we were continually keeping an eagle eye out for Gypsy and almost resigned ourselves into thinking that our paths would never cross again. We still lived in hope though, and we had a couple of false alarms mistaking similar dogs for her. They could very well have been her offspring!

We visited some of the restaurants we enjoyed from last time, found some new ones and visited several different parts of the island. Having heard so much about the infamous 'full moon parties' on a nearby island called

Koh Pha Ngan, we decided to catch a boat from Bophut one morning (known as the Fisherman's Village as indicated on a huge sign suspended over the entrance) and spend the day there. Our intention was not to stay for the 'celebrations' knowing that it was notorious for drug-taking and drunken behaviour on a grand scale, particularly among the younger element, and we were well out of that age group.

We enjoyed the beautiful beach and various bars before leaving the island late afternoon. We were tempted at one point to stay longer to see what all the fuss was about, but would then have had a problem over getting accommodation. Sleeping on the beach like most of the partygoers was simply not our style. We decided that we would plan another visit and arrange to stop overnight, but that never happened. We have since watched TV documentaries about this world-famous event, and to be honest, we were glad it did not materialise.

Approximately half way back across the Andaman Sea our motor launch suddenly started shuddering and gradually slowed down to a complete stop. Our pilot radioed to Bophut for someone to come out and attend to the problem, so we had no option but to keep floating in the one spot for over an hour. What was amusing in hindsight was the fact that other boats were passing by us, with passengers laughing and waving to us as though we were there out of choice! No question of them towing us back! It was quite relaxing though, until someone noticed a lone shark fin breaking the surface in different places around us, with 'Jaws' probably licking its lips in anticipation!

"Marie! Will you stop dangling your toes in the water! You're attracting it and you've only just bought those sandals. I definitely won't be paying for another pair!"

called one man who was from Liverpool to his wife (a typical 'scouser' sense of humour!), which lightened the mood a little. We were relieved to be rescued fairly quickly and returned to Koh Samui on another boat, living to drink Mekong another day.

Speaking of the drink Mekong, I would like to elaborate. This is a Thai spirit usually sold as a 'whiskey set', which is served up in a half bottle, a steel bucket full of ice cubes and a bottle of coca cola. Quite a potent drink that someone told us had formaldehyde as one of the ingredients! I was informed it was a type of embalming fluid! I don't know how true that is, but I had some very strange dreams afterwards. One such dream had me sitting in a recording studio helping to produce Kylie Minogue's latest album! I could vividly experience sitting beside her discussing different songs being recorded and hearing them, as though we had been friends for life.

The downside which Phil suffered was a nightmare where every single person walking past him was completely swathed in bandages, like Mummies! He was glad to wake up from it and said we would have to drink less of the Mekong from now on, which I was in full agreement with. We sometimes drank the other Thai speciality called Sang Thip, which was rum served in the same way but didn't seem as potent. Sometimes for a change we drank ice cold locally brewed beers like Singha or Chang which were brewed in Bangkok.

Another venue we learnt about from the Samui Welcome magazine was a place called Magic Alambics Garden Bar. It was owned by Michel and Elisa from France and was situated not far from the Na Muang waterfalls. They mainly produced and offered various flavoured rums like lime, pineapple, coconut and orange and we could not resist a visit and that extended to a second one! Why waste a good opportunity with drinks like that on the menu?

One of our favourite restaurants on the main road in Chaweng was in a massive building with a thatched roof. It was called the Chaweng Food Market and was split into several different sections. Part of it was self-service and the rest 'a la carte' and dining areas were inside and out. The manager, Tin, hailed from Burma, so much of the food on offer came from there, and we were tempted to go twice as it was very close to our hotel. There was always entertainment from 8pm in the evening from Thai and Filipino bands which all helped with the special ambience. Although we were 'all-inclusive' we often still enjoyed trying other places some evenings just to ring the changes. Going to the same place every night does become monotonous no matter how tempting or varied the menu is, specially over a few weeks.

As you can imagine, Koh Samui has an extremely wide range of restaurants covering worldwide cuisine and the most popular ones without a doubt, were those situated along the beaches. Wriggling your bare toes in fine white sand while you browse the menu has to be one of life's little pleasures. A favourite of ours, the Sea Shell, had actually positioned their chairs and tables on a raft which was resting in the shallow water. We could experience waves lapping underneath the wooden planks. Obviously, if there was any sign of sea turbulence the tables and chairs were positioned back on the beach. Customers floating out to sea would not have been a good selling point for the restaurant! Their menus were crammed with typical Thai food and juicy burgers and being surrounded by myriads of tree lights only enhanced the experience. About twenty yards away from that was our favourite, The Ark bar which featured amazing DJs playing mainly dance music but more chill out music as the evening went on, as mentioned earlier.

We sometimes ate in the town and became attached to a very typical Thai restaurant which all the locals frequented. The decor was very basic and because we could not pronounce the name, we nicknamed it the 'Formica'. Once you got past the 'tear gas' cloud (chillies being fried), you could see all the food being cooked in front of you and you sat at Formica topped tables on white plastic chairs. The cost was considerably cheaper than the main dining places but the atmosphere and the cuisine could not have been more authentic. As 'farangs' (foreigners) we integrated quite well once we had dined there several times, as we used to have our lunches there some days. Our favourite meals were Thai red or green curries, Pad Thai, chicken in peanut sauce and tempura battered shrimps with sweet chilli sauce. My mouth is watering at the mere thought of it all!

We were sitting in a cafe bar one afternoon off the main street in Chaweng, when I heard a young guy speaking in a familiar accent. To be precise he was from Merseyside like ourselves or was what many consider as a 'scouser'! This term comes from the name of a particular dish called scouse which consists of potatoes, onions and carrots in a stew with either lamb or beef. Apparently, this dish was originally brought to Liverpool by North European sailors and was called lobskause (lobscouse).

I asked him where he was from and he said Crosby, which was a town close to the River Mersey and Liverpool and by coincidence where Phil lived when he was younger. Alec later moved to Macclesfield where we presently lived in the village of Bollington. It transpired that he lived on

Koh Samui for five months of each year between November and March, approximately. He funded this extended holiday by working at Atax as a taxi driver during the summer months, then staying in the Elephant Bungalows on Chaweng beach on self-catering. I told him that I was convinced I had seen him before and he said "You are a video cameraman, aren't you? I'm sure I have driven you to a few weddings around Cheshire". Well the penny dropped and everything fell into place. The chance of that happening was so amazing and it is indeed a small world sometimes! We arranged to meet up another day for an Indian meal before we went home.

Alec was fascinated with our story of Gypsy and hoped that we would be reunited with her on this holiday, though he thought it was highly unlikely on an island of that size. We gave him our email address and asked him to contact us when back in the UK. This he did in late summer and we spent a very enjoyable afternoon in the Jolly Sailor pub in Macclesfield over a few pints. Also, a new Thai restaurant had recently opened in the town, so we had to try that, of course. He told us then that he was eventually moving on to another Island called Ko Lanta near Koh Phi Phi, as he had been going to Koh Samui for four years and felt it was time to try somewhere different.

On our last Thai holiday in Koh Phi Phi we took a boat trip there, but it seemed to lack what we enjoyed about Koh Samui. Alec was certainly a very adventurous young man, as he always travelled on his own. We did meet up with him another couple of times back in England and on the final time he said he had met someone on home turf and was prepared to settle down, so his long stays in Thailand would be coming to an end. He said this did not rule out going back for short holidays though after he was married, as Thailand had played a significant part in his life. I was hoping he would ask me to film their wedding but unfortunately, he did not!

In a local side street restaurant one lunchtime, I was calmly sitting at a table waiting to be served, when suddenly I felt myself gradually sinking downwards on one side. Next moment there was an ear-splitting crack and there I was flat on my back with my legs in the air like an upturned beetle! The chair had completely collapsed and was in two pieces and OBVIOUSLY very poorly constructed!! When the ripple of laughter had subsided, a concerned looking waiter appeared. 'Big, too big" he announced, far too loudly for my liking. I said, with tongue in cheek, "Sorry but I didn't come here to be insulted. We'll go somewhere else, Phil." I realised right away the irony of what I had said and also how funny it must have been to the other diners! The humour was lost on the waiter though, who had a deadpan expression on his face the whole time, which is quite characteristic of the Asian countries. It did cause me to think seriously about my weight being much higher than it ought to be though! Time to start yet another diet when I get home was my decision!

DRCS first Clinic with Chinai standing

Dog and Cat Rescue Samui Foundation logo (formerly DRCS)

Me with Gypsy on water bed

Our favourite beach bar- the Reggae Pub

Thai dogs get passports to beat rabies

May 1, 2001
Web posted at: 6:30 AM EDT (1030 GMT)

By Staff and wire reports

BANGKOK, Thailand -- Thailand plans to issue passports to dog owners who want to take their dogs to rabies-free zones in a bid to ensure the safety of tourists.

Stray dogs are the prime cause of rabies infections in Thailand

So far only two islands in Thailand are declared rabies-free zones -- Koh Samui and Koh Samet.

Koh Samui was chosen because it had not had a single report of rabies since 1985. All dogs are vaccinated against the rabies virus in the resort island.

Valid for five years

Passports would be valid for five years and include information on rabies vaccinations, record of ownership and a traveling record, a local Bangkok newspaper reported.

Fifty people died of rabies in Thailand last year. This year 12 people have already died.

Many of rabies victims get the disease from dog bites, especially from stray dogs. In Thailand, a predominantly Buddhist country, the killing of homeless dogs is generally opposed.

The campaign was initiated by the Livestock Development Department with the Communicable Diseases Control Department, the Tourism Authority and the Thai Red Cross Society.

Rabies info

Absent arachnid from Na Muang waterfall (maybe)

We first met Gypsy on this beach

Werner, Brigitte & Phil

Brigitte, Werner and I at their home

Waiting for their tick games

We spent many nights here

VETERINARY HEALTH CERTIFICATE

SPECIES: K-9
NAME: GYPSY
BREED/COLOUR: MIXED / Black
AGE: 1-1-98
SEX: ♀ (o-hyst, cm-15)
OWNERS NAME: Mr. Robert T. Cooper
ADDRESS: 9 Sowcar Way Bollington.
Macclesfield Cheshire SK 10 SQW England.

TODAY I HAVE EXAMINED THE ABOVE DISCRIBED ANIMAL. IT SHOWS NO CLINICAL SIGNS OF RABIES OR OTHER INFECTIOUS OR CONTAGIOUS DISEASE AND IS, IN MY OPINION, FIT FOR TRAVEL. THIS CERTIFICATE IS VALID FOR 10 DAYS FROM DATE OF SIGNATURE.

VETERINARIAN:	Dr. SOMSAK SRISUTHAM (DVM.)
DATE:	2 - MAY - 2000
SIGNATURE:	

NOTE: THIS HEALTH CERTIFICATE IS ONLY VALID WHILST ACCOMPANIED BY THE VACCINATION RECORDS OF THE ANIMAL DISCRIBED ABOVE.

Vet Dr.Somsak's examination certificate

Phil with Gypsy at the clinic

Phil with Rhino

PATONG BEACH HOTEL & BAAN SAMUI RESORT

Dear Sir

This is the second letter that I am forced to write to you regarding the dogs.

It is <u>not</u> hotel policy to allow the dogs inside the hotel and especially <u>not</u> in the rooms. It is unhygenic and it is unfair to the next guests who occupy your room. It also causes additional work for the housekeeping department.

Therefore I regret to inform you, we will be charging you 500B for damage to the bed sheets ie. dog hair which is difficult to clean.

We will continue to charge you 500B a day if the dog continues to sleep in your room.

Please understand it is also unfair to the dog who will visit this room after you leave, looking for it's "owner", causing unnecessary stress for the dog and possibly the next guests who may not like dogs.

Yours Sincerely

Kerry Bennett   Guest Relations

Baan Samui Hotel letter

Ministry of Agriculture Fisheries and Food
Scottish Office Agriculture and Fisheries Department
Welsh Office Agriculture Department

ANIMAL HEALTH ACT 1981
RABIES (IMPORTATION OF DOGS, CATS AND OTHER MAMMALS) ORDER 1974 (AS AMENDED)

Certificate of Vaccination against Rabies

1. Name and address of owner of animal

   MR R COOPER
   % CHAGCOW KENNEL

2. Quarantine kennels at which vaccinated

   CHAGCOW QUARANTINE KENNEL
   NR CALOW
   CHESTERFIELD
   DERBYS   S44 5AN

3. Particulars of animal:
   - (i) Licence number: D/0034299
   - (ii) Date of entry into quarantine: 12-5-00
   - (iii) Country of origin: THAILAND
   - (iv) Name of animal: GYPSY
   - (v) Breed: LABRADOR CROSS DOG
   - (vi) Sex: FEMALE
   - (vii) Age: 2
   - (viii) Colour: BLACK
   - (ix) Distinctive marks:

4. Particulars of vaccination. (Where 2 doses of a vaccine are required, particulars of both doses should be given.)

	First dose of vaccine	Second dose of vaccine (if applicable)
(i) Date of vaccination	13/5/00	
(ii) Name of vaccine	RABISIN	
(iii) Name of supplier	N.V.S.	
(iv) Batch number	L633 82	
(v) Expiry date	19/04/2002	

   This is to certify that I, the undersigned, have vaccinated the animal described at (3) with the inactivated rabies vaccine at (4).

   Signed .... RCVS Date 23/06/00
   Name in BLOCK LETTERS   I K TAYLOR

   COPY FOR RETENTION BY OWNER OF ANIMAL

   ID 68 (Revised 2/92)

Rabies vaccination certificate

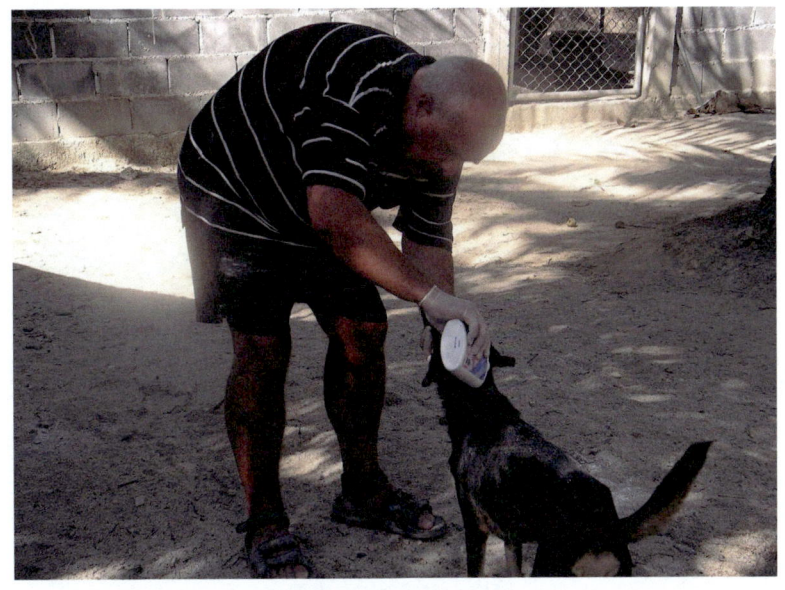

Applying tick powder

Mai on Chaweng beach

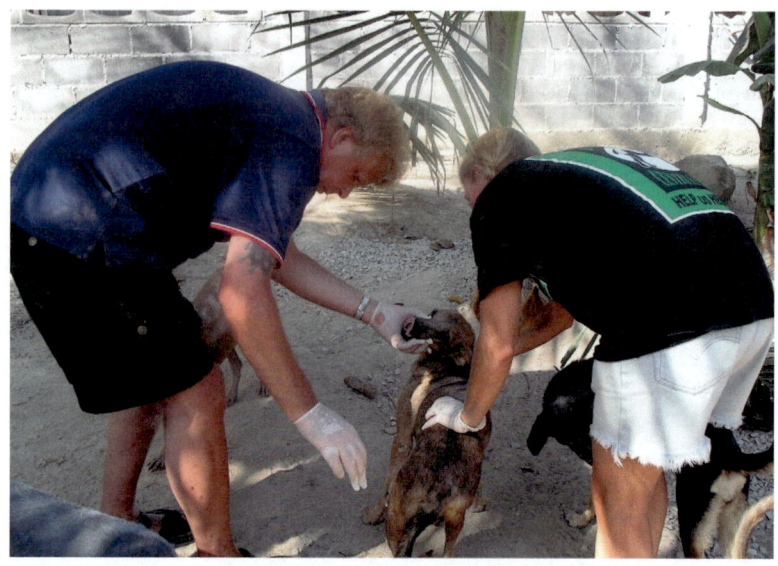
Phil with a volunteer

Me with Monica at the DRCS

Me with Gypsy and beach trader, Chaweng beach

Me with Gypsy afloat

MINISTRY OF AGRICULTURE & CO-OPERATIVES
DEPARTMENT OF LIVESTOCK DEVELOPMENT, THAILAND.
VETERINARY HEALTH CERTIFICATE

No. _____
ORIGINAL

Export of Animals & Birds

Name & Address of Exporter	Name & Address of Importer
MR. ROBERT COOPER BANGKOK, THAILAND.	MR. ROBERT COOPER UNITED KINGDOM.

Number	Species	Breed or Trade Name
1 HEAD **********	CANINE **********	NAME: GYPSY BREED: MIXED SEX: FEMALE AGE: 2 YRS. COLOR: BLACK ******************

I hereby certify that animals or birds specified above has/have been examined and found to the best of my knowledge and believed to be free from any evidence of infectious or contagious diseases.

REMARKS:

I further certify that the animal(s) is/are vaccinated

Against   RABIES   on   30 MAR 2000   Exp Date   30 MAR 2001
              ****

Signed _____
Name Dr. NIRUNDORN AUNGTRAGOOLSUK BSc.,D.V.M
Veterinary Official Chief Veterinary Officer
Bangkok Airport Animal Quarantine Station
Official stamp.   Date 1 0 MAY 2000

Official letter from the Ministry of Agriculture

Brigitte and manager Wit

Cocktails on Maenam beach

Happy together on Chaweng beach

Surprise Reunion

'To us, a miracle had just taken place'

All the while we were enjoying our holiday, we were still haunted by thoughts of Gypsy and wondering where she could possibly be, especially whilst we were on the beach. One thing we did grow to love was the beach community, forever wandering along the shore selling all manner of things, mostly food. They were not at all pressurising and some of them were a pleasure to sit with, particularly if they spoke a little English.

One such lady called Mai cooked chicken pieces and corn on the cob on a small barbecue. She loved us attempting to teach her English words and she tried to teach us some of the Thai phrases, but that was far more complicated. I think she learned much more from us! The Thai language is very difficult, so we tried to learn a few basic words like 'sawasdee ka' and 'arun sawat' which strangely both mean 'hello' or 'good morning'. Just to be more confusing, they can also be used as 'good afternoon'!

An elderly fisherman used to sit beside us sometimes, cooking freshly caught red snapper and sea bass along with sweet potato fries. This was useful around 2pm when our breakfasts had become history. One enterprising young man presented us with a tray containing what appeared to be deep fried shrimps. On closer inspection, I thought shrimps don't have wings? The guy explained what they were in Thai and the English translation was fried crickets and grasshoppers! It was very daunting to me but Phil plucked up the courage to taste one. The grimace on his face convinced me to renege on those. "Just like crispy balsa wood!" was his description of them, though I did wonder when he had ever tried that! Another selection was obviously crunchy cockroaches, which he didn't try and neither did I!

A lady selling various types of fruit persuaded us to try 'durian' fruit one day but the odour it gave off was repulsive to put it mildly. The taste wasn't as bad as the smell, but we decided not to bother with that again. Another memory of beach life was listening repeatedly to the words "You massaaart?"("You want massage?") coming from the pretty Thai masseuses in their primitive little cabins nestled on the sand. This was very popular with many tourists but we never participated.

A pattern of weather emerged over several days whereby each afternoon around 4pm there would be roughly half an hour of torrential rain with thunder, lightning and strong winds. We would first notice a dark purplish-grey strip on the horizon gradually widening as it approached the island. A sure sign that made everyone evacuate the roughening water and head for shelter in a beach bar. The owners would quickly drag large sheets of Perspex over the entrance to prevent potential flooding. Once the storm had passed the sun appeared again and everything dried within 30 minutes. Sometimes a second storm would follow in quick succession. We always felt it was a welcome diversion from just lounging on the beach and actually found it to be rather exciting, I must admit.

Unfortunately, these freak storms played havoc with the internet, and of course Brigitte suffered severe consequences. Sometime these 'blips' lasted for days or even a week and were especially annoying when the latest newsletter was being produced! Aside from these storms, the weather was predominantly fine and always around the same temperature of 30-33 degrees even overnight. The air conditioning was essential and sometimes we would happily wander round a supermarket for 10 minutes, just to escape the heat after we had left the beach.

About five days into our holiday, we decided to take a walk further along Chaweng beach and bought a bag of dry dog food to distribute amongst any stray dogs we found on the way. Whilst doing this, a middle-aged couple came up to us and the woman said, "We think it's wonderful what you are doing for the dogs. It must be costing you a bomb and wearing you out as well in this heat. We've been feeding a lovely black dog outside our hotel each morning. We always sneak out bacon and sausages from the breakfast buffet and she loves it!" She described this dog to us as black with white paws and told us that they were staying in the Blue Lagoon Hotel about a couple of hundred yards further down the beach. This description rang a bell immediately and we briefly told them about first meeting with Gypsy the year before and we had returned hoping to find her again. They wished us luck and we headed in that direction with hearts beating fast and more than a little hopeful.

We tried to be rational in thinking, it was probably just similar to many dogs of that breed and not the one we were hoping to find. It was exciting though, as we got closer to the hotel. Near the entrance, we noticed a black dog curled up in a ball, in a hole in the sand wearing a tan collar like the one we bought the previous year! When we were within a couple of yards Phil called out quietly, "Gypsy!" After momentarily looking bewildered, she responded immediately by leaping towards us, making this famous 'mooing' sound that we'd heard so often. She went berserk with excitement and proceeded to run round in circles barking at the different people sprawled on the beach as if to say, "Look who's come back to see me". We just could not believe our good fortune in finding her again, when deep down we had thought we were expecting the impossible. It was a very emotional reunion which even affected complete strangers sunbathing on the beach. They were amazed to learn we had made friends with her over a year before and that she still remembered us. To us, a miracle had just taken place, so what do we do now?

What Next for Gypsy?

'You are best just slipping away quietly
before any of the police come'

Finding Gypsy again put a whole different slant on the holiday, as we realised that we would not be able to take her back to our hotel room at all. What would we do after being with her each day? It did not bear thinking about and how we would cope with leaving her on the island for a second time, which seemed inevitable. We had to decide on a plan of action, as the first full day with her was coming to a close. We were a considerable distance from the Baan Samui Hotel, so we hit on the idea to ask a bar owner to keep her until we'd jumped into a 'songthaew' or 'tuk-tuk' (like an open-backed taxi). This was the only practical thing to do at that time but we were not sure it would always work. Some days she would momentarily vanish off down the beach with her dog friends, so we grasped those opportunities to return to our hotel, which solved that problem for part of our holiday.

The bar we usually chose was also a French restaurant owned by a young woman called Martine and her then partner Pasquale. She was originally from St. Malo and several years before had decided to travel around Thailand for a year or so backpacking. Loving Koh Samui so much, she invested a windfall from her Grandmother's will in property on Chaweng beach. Originally opened with her boyfriend Antoine, after 18 months or so he returned to France to work as a chef in Marseille. Now established for three years, 'Panache' was doing well, so this place was a life saver with regard to Gypsy as we could leave her there whenever we wanted. We of course always indulged in a couple of glasses of wine whilst there and occasionally a meal, so we were all winners.

Another safe haven further along the beach was with an Australian guy called Benjamin. He kept Gypsy with him a few times when we returned to our hotel. It was only a beach shack which he cleverly called 'Ozzie's', but he was a fascinating man telling us tales of his travels around the world. He looked rather like Crocodile Dundee with his large floppy hat and his weather-beaten face. He had basic fare on offer like coffee and bottles of ice-cold beer, but produced some very tasty waffles served with ice cream. On the sand in front of his bar, local Thai boys would join some hotel guests to play volleyball most days. We even joined in once but found the combination of high temperatures and our ages to be too tiring for us. We preferred to be spectators rather than participants, but at least we had made the effort!

As we anticipated having to leave Gypsy on the island again, we tentatively approached Benjamin, asking him if he would adopt Gypsy when we had gone back home. Well, his reaction wasn't what we expected. He nodded over to another dog which belonged to him, laughed and said, "You've got to be joking!' Feeding that bastard over there is enough to cope with matey! He can be a bloody nuisance sometimes." We were shocked at his attitude, so in hindsight, it was just as well he didn't agree. There was no way we could have trusted him and that was the last time we visited his bar. So we still had that dilemma to resolve.

One afternoon, we were relaxing with Gypsy on the sand near the Blue Lagoon, when a rather mangey looking dog decided to place himself down beside us. We gave him some dog biscuits and a bowl of water and he was quite content to sit there, obviously enjoying the attention and the food and drink. Suddenly he started growling at a couple of young Thai men who were walking along the water's edge. One of them attempted to kick him out of the way and the dog retaliated by biting one of his legs! The next thing we knew a whole crowd had gathered around the pair, mostly local Thai people. They were furiously jabbering at each other and an Australian guy told us they were going to inform the police, which might result in us having our passports confiscated. He said, "I don't want to alarm you, but I understand some of what they are saying. They know your dog didn't actually bite the man, but are blaming yours because of the association. They have taken the man to hospital and are even discussing that you would have to pay the injured man 'lots of money'! You are best just slipping away quietly before any of the police come." This indeed was a frightening thought.

We thanked him for his advice as at this point, we have to admit we were extremely concerned at this disturbing information. He said that something similar had happened a month earlier and the owners of a dog had been taken to Nathon Police Station and had had their passports confiscated. They somehow extricated about £700 from the couple for their return, spurred on by over-exaggerating local Thais out to make money. This side of the Thai culture we had not seen before and it shocked us. This guy was only trying to help us, but it did make us extremely anxious.

Despite this unexpected and frightening turn of events, Phil and I packed up our towels, put Gypsy on her lead and proceeded to walk along the sand in the opposite direction as calmly as we could, even though we were both trembling inside. Our scruffy dog friend had already fled the scene and had disappeared further along the beach. There was no point in attempting to talk our way out of this situation, mainly because of the language barrier. We thought it was more sensible to just leave the scene as discreetly as possible. We should have gone to 'Panache', but we would have had to walk back amongst the irate crowd that had gathered. We must have walked about a mile up the beach before settling down on a quiet stretch of sand where we tried to calm down. Within minutes, a young beach trader appeared, pointed at Gypsy and shouted "Bad, black dog," when she had not done anything wrong! We realised that he had followed us and very soon it would be on the beach front grapevine.

When he had disappeared, we decided we would have to leave the beach by scrambling through the undergrowth and towering palm trees as quickly as possible, in the direction of the main road. Eventually, we found a roadside bar to take refuge in, very dishevelled and extremely tired. We sat there with a few cold beers for a couple of hours till darkness fell. The bar owner, who was incidentally from Amsterdam (where we had visited many times), agreed to temporarily look after Gypsy for us, so we were able to return to our hotel to reflect on what had happened earlier that day. It was now a very concerning scenario. We had very little sleep that night wondering what dramas the following day would bring.

With our hearts in our mouths, we were very apprehensive searching for Gypsy that morning. We walked the length and breadth of Chaweng beach and eventually found her close to the Samui Natien hotel. We spent a few hours there, thankful that there were no further unpleasant developments relating to the previous day. Late that afternoon, while Gypsy was busy running in and out of the sea with her canine friends, we decided to head back to our hotel in a tuk-tuk. We were mulling over which restaurant we would eat at that night, when all of a sudden, we received the shock of our lives!

After a few minutes of traveling along Chaweng's busy coast road, roughly 3 kilometres in length, Gypsy's bobbing head appeared, weaving between the heavy traffic on the road behind us! Every few moments or so, we temporarily lost sight of her behind cars and bikes, so we asked the driver to slow down so she could catch us up. We then spotted her about fifteen yards behind us sitting on a street corner, very out of breath. Like a wolf, she had thrown her head back and was howling long and mournfully. She had obviously exhausted herself and was unable to keep chasing our taxi. We stopped it immediately, paid the driver and within one minute had decided that some way or another, we would have to take her back to England. How we would arrange that was a complete mystery to us, but with only one week left before finishing our holiday, we had to start the process right away and not waste a moment.

Life-Changing Decision

'It was yet another stumbling
block to surmount'

Through Gypsy's sheer determination, we had now come to realise, that to leave her behind again was absolutely out of the question There was no doubt in our minds that she had adopted us and wanted us to care for her from now on. The thought of her still living there, foraging for food, being involved in dogfights and possibly being poisoned by hotel staff made us completely determined to take her away from all that. We attempted to call Brigitte but could not make any connection. We decided we had no option but to visit Martine and ask her if she could keep Gypsy overnight till we could work out a plan of action. She very kindly agreed. We spent most of that night discussing this difficult situation and our options.

The following morning, our first step was to telephone Brigitte at the Samui Dog Rescue. We asked her if it was possible to keep Gypsy at the clinic, as we were intending to arrange her departure from Thailand, for the distant shores of England. We knew it had put her in the firing line and she was very reluctant at first. We of course knew the clinic was designated solely for the sick and injured animals being cared for there, plus the ones to be spayed and vaccinated. Space was at a premium, but she eventually agreed to letting her stay in the kitchen, after a long and persuasive telephone conversation with Ulrike from Germany. She was around thirty years old and currently on the island with her boyfriend and we spent several nights dining and drinking with them. Ulrike was a regular helper and donator who spent most of her holidays on Koh Samui for that purpose.

This proved to be a traumatic experience for everyone. I still have a vision in my mind of seeing a huge pan full of chicken heads bubbling away on the stove in the upstairs kitchen, which was a very inexpensive way of feeding the dogs, but nutritious! Gypsy several times managed to sneak out of the glass front entrance if left ajar after we had taken her back from her daily walks along the beach. Thankfully Chinai, one of Brigitte's staff, managed to chase after her and bring her back on each occasion. In the clinic, Gypsy was also quite adept at jumping up onto the office desk, accidently stepping on the stamp pad and leaving a trail of blue paw prints everywhere! Brigitte was not amused!

Phil, being a catholic, wanted to visit the Church of St. Anne in the middle of the island, to pray for Gypsy's hopeful eventual transference to England and for the welfare of the other dogs who would be staying and going nowhere. He felt so much better after doing this, so then we began exploring the surrounding village. It was definitely one of the poorest areas we had witnessed, with many stray cats and dogs wandering about, some in a disturbing condition. We mentioned it to Brigitte when we arrived back in Chaweng so that some sort of treatment could be arranged to help the situation there.

We noticed a small open air 'supermarket', for want of a better word, with a 'cafe' area and sat down on two rickety wooden chairs next to a rusty oil drum (table). We played safe by ordering cans of coke rather than risk coffees in some rather grubby looking mugs. We were flabbergasted to see how randomly the goods were displayed, like bottles of cooking oil standing right next to bleach and washing powder on the same shelf as breakfast cereals. Jars of coffee were leaning against shampoo bottles and shaving cream propping up bunches of bananas. Waitrose it wasn't! That certainly was an eye-opener, but perfectly normal to those living in that community. Our local Tesco at home was like Harrods in comparison!

Incidentally, on our next visit to the island Brigitte took us to see the new superstore Tesco Lotus, which was so enormous. Yes, they get everywhere!

In this same village, a small outdoor stall was crammed with different sized plant pots and ornaments of animals and birds. Phil thought we ought to buy something to take back to England, so we began searching through the items on display. Everything was precariously balanced, so we carefully manoeuvred our way around, picking up various objects. We settled on a two-foot-high heron with a red beak, intended for our garden. Very pleased with our choice, we offered our money to the tiny lady standing nearby. All of a sudden, behind us we heard a loud clatter and realised we had just been picking up plant pots from this display. It was now a crumbled heap of alabaster! We very embarrassingly offered to pay for all the damage which was only equivalent to £20, thank goodness. The bird was only £3 initially, and has amazingly survived over twenty years through all weathers, so we certainly had our money's worth out of that!

As well as the famous island Koh Pha Ngan where the notorious full moon parties took place, Koh Samui held a more civilised half-moon party held in the centre of Chaweng beach. Apart from several bands playing mostly reggae music, there were firework displays, fire dancers who juggled flaming torches and, most special of all, candlelit lanterns released into the night sky, a truly spectacular sight as they headed towards the stars. These magical moments have forever been stamped indelibly in our memories.

One morning on the beach near our hotel we saw one of our elderly beach seller ladies. She sat on the sand next to us to talk and then mentioned Gypsy. "I see you every day with that black dog. She loves you very much but she will die when you go home. She won't eat or drink water. I tell you that because I know!" and winked. I took both of her hands and said, "She won't die because we are hoping to take her over to England in a few days' time!" Well, the next moment, tears were running down her cheeks which immediately set us off! She said "I so happy! You are such kind men so I give you some chicken wings for free!" What very special and emotional moments we shared then, which we just didn't expect. The chicken wings went down a treat with sweet chili sauce and Chang beers!

Strangely enough, when we were having an evening in the resort of Lamai further down the coast, we mentioned to a young Thai girl in a bar that we were to about to take a dog back to England. She shrieked with laughter and said "Why you not love me and care for me. You take me to England, then I will be very happy!" No doubt she would have been, but I didn't have the heart to say we preferred Gypsy!

Whilst Gypsy was in residence at the clinic, we were extremely busy browsing the internet for quarantine kennels in England and all the other official bodies we had to contact, including the Ministry of Agriculture. We were exhausted jumping through all the different hoops to try and make sense of the worrying situation that lay in front of us. We discovered Calagran Quarantine Kennels was the nearest one to where we lived and this was based just outside Chesterfield. Of course, the main priority was for her to have all the necessary injections required before leaving the island, so this was arranged with Dr. Somsak Srithusam, the Vet.

Financially, it was impossible for us at that time to produce all the money needed to pay for Gypsy's two flights plus the Vet's fees but Brigitte and her husband, Werner generously loaned us thousands of Thai Baht to cover the costs. This was based on her weight, as the airport authorities had decided she must travel as 'cargo'! Her flights from Koh Samui to Bangkok, then onto London were going to cost in the region of £400-£500, which was equivalent to what we paid each for our return flights!

After countless telephone calls, faxes and emails, we were under the impression we had everything in place for her long journey to the UK. Our flight was on the 5th May and to make absolutely certain Gypsy was booked on both of our flights, I rang the airport to confirm that she would be accompanying us. I was devastated to learn that she would not be able to travel on the same aircraft as us because she had no export licence and it would take at least three or four days to acquire one! We had an import licence, but for some strange reason, we had not been advised about needing the other one or we had just overlooked it. We received this information approximately three hours before we were due to leave our hotel for the airport!

This was the most horrendous news we could possibly have received and time was rapidly running out. We both had a sinking feeling, that all our efforts to achieve something almost impossible were about to completely unravel. We made the decision to telephone Calagran Kennels in Chesterfield to tell them they would not be collecting Gypsy from Heathrow Airport after all. It took ages to connect, but Mike Binks told me that a new minister had been appointed and he does everything by the book, so we would just have to be patient. He then advised me to telephone an Irish lady called Liz Mulqueen at Crown Worldwide Handling Agents in Bangkok, to see if she could help us with our plight. When we eventually made contact, she explained that at that time of day and at such short notice, she was unable to contact anyone that could resolve the situation. She suggested that we would have to fly home as planned and during our journey she would move heaven and earth with regard to Gypsy's exodus. There was nothing we could do but to put all our trust in her, but it was yet another stumbling block to surmount.

We were obviously very unhappy at the prospect of our dog having to stay behind at the Dog Rescue Clinic, particularly with her track record of escaping whenever possible. Brigitte told us they could not guarantee they would be able to catch her if she escaped again. That was something else to worry about! If we had not used our flights, it would have cost us well over £1000 to purchase new tickets, plus of course any accommodation we might need. This was totally out of the question, so we had to take the advice from Liz and reluctantly return home. I was committed to returning to England anyway, to fulfil a wedding booking at home at Shrigley Hall the day after our flight back. She told us to check our email as soon as we arrived home, which would be in approximately 22 hours' time, taking into account the five hours time difference, the change of plane in Bangkok and the two hour stop for refuelling in Switzerland. Also, a final flight to Manchester from London Heathrow.

Gypsy seemed to sense that something was wrong and became very agitated, even though she had been given a tranquiliser. We had bought her a cage to travel in for approximately £100 and lined it with one of our beach towels, so she would have something familiar that belonged to us to sleep on. While I was speaking to Mike, I heard in the background that Brigitte was ranting on to Phil about Gypsy. "We have never told you that every day

Gypsy has cried and cried each time you left her, for hours on end, because her heart was breaking. She has run away several times. She has bitten through a rope and her crying and squealing kept setting all the other dogs off barking. The noise has been deafening at times! One day we nearly decided to just let her run away, but when I thought of your love for her, we just could not do it so we just sent Chinai after her once again. The times he has had to do that! 'We always anticipated having problems sending dogs to England, which is why we have never tried to till now'. We can send as many dogs as we like to Germany without a problem! They just walk off the plane with their dog and take them straight home."

Werner then started shouting at Brigitte, telling her to calm down, then someone dropped a metal tray containing medical instruments on the tiled floor with an incredible clatter! Next thing, Gypsy started to howl, which made all the other dogs start barking their heads off! You have never heard such a cacophony of noise! It was just like being in a madhouse! Mike heard much of this while he was listening to me and said it would all work out eventually and we would laugh about it one day! That was hard to foresee at the time, but in hindsight it does now seem rather a comical situation!

After we had said our tearful goodbyes to Gypsy, we reluctantly climbed into Werner's car and headed back to our hotel to collect our luggage. Part of the way to the airport, we remembered that we had rolls of film to be collected from the processors, so we had to make a detour to get them. Feeling so despondent on the way to the airport, Phil, Werner and I drowned our sorrows in a bottle of Mekong in the airport lounge. Werner had tears in his eyes when he hugged us both and jokingly said "I will be in trouble with Brigitte now for drinking and keeping her waiting at the clinic!" (There were no drink/driving laws over in Thailand at that time). It was a combined feeling of 'déjà vu' and feeling merry, as we climbed the aircraft steps just over a year from the last time we left Koh Samui. It seemed to us that we had been thwarted in our efforts to take Gypsy home and were both of the opinion that once we had left the island again, the chances of her leaving Thailand would be very slim. We would just have to wait and see what fate held in store for us all and hope that Liz could perform a miracle while we were flying back to England without her, for the second time.

Success at Last

'Our dreams of bringing Gypsy back to
our country had very nearly evaporated'

All kinds of negative thoughts went through our minds as our plane to Bangkok drew further away from Koh Samui. Facing the challenge of going through customs in an airport like Bangkok is traumatic at the best of times, with the vast enormity of it. To give you some idea of the size, at that time there were 120 immigration desks and 22 luggage carousels! We half-heartedly wandered around the King Power duty-free shop looking for souvenirs and some bottles of spirits to take back, but our minds were still firmly entrenched on the island we had just left. We gave Mike Binks a quick call to advise him that we had made contact with Liz and it was now in her hands. He was quite confident that she would do everything in her power and told us not to worry. "Easier said than done," I said! Once we had boarded our flight from Bangkok to London Heathrow, there would be no way of ensuring Gypsy would ever leave Thailand.

The previous year we had also flown with Thai Airways. When flying with that airline, a unique touch is that every passenger is presented with a tall, see-through box containing a bunch of Thai orchids on the return flight. Once we had settled down in our seats, our minds were overflowing with questions that needed to be answered. Perhaps we were being cruel attempting to remove Gypsy from her natural environment? If we did succeed in transporting her to England, would she settle in happily with our other dogs? How would our climate affect a dog used to permanent average temperatures of over 30 degrees? All of these thoughts and more kept haunting us on our long journey home. All through the flight, waves of anguish kept washing over us when our minds flashed back to the moment when we all separated, perhaps maybe forever? Seeking solace in several glasses of our favourite spirit, Jack Daniel's, only accentuated the heartache we were suffering.

Matters weren't helped by the fact of having to break our journey and go through the Swiss customs. Of course we had a carrier bag full of duty-free spirits, which the officials said would have to be confiscated! We were assured by the young sales assistant in the duty-free shop in Bangkok that we would be allowed to take them to the UK, but apparently not. I was so angry that I could not help saying, "I hope you all enjoy your boozy party when you come off duty later on." The lady officer retorted, "You be careful what you say, sir...it's all going to be destroyed, I'm afraid; those are the rules!" Well, that made us feel even worse when we envisaged all that whiskey and vodka disappearing down a plughole instead of our throats!

I was very tempted to reply, "That's a likely story," but thought better of it as the customs lady was like 'Bea' Smith, one of the guards from the Australian TV series 'Cell Block H!' Our demeanour went even more downhill after that. No dog, no alcohol! Could it get any worse?

On arrival at Heathrow airport, nearly six thousand miles from Thailand, our dreams of bringing Gypsy back to our country had very nearly evaporated. Because we were no longer 'on the premises', we had visions of her escaping from the dog clinic and Chinai or any of the other workers not bothering to try and catch her. While we were on Koh Samui, the bond we had made with the staff there, particularly Chinai, made them feel obligated to keep retrieving her from the beach, which was highly frustrating for them. Now we were so far away, there would not perhaps be the same incentive, and that would be the end of all the efforts we had made. Luckily, Chinai did keep a watchful eye on her and managed to collect Gypsy from

Chaweng beach twice, when she fled from the rescue centre. He deserved a medal.

On our journey from Heathrow to Manchester Airport, via British Airways, we were both extremely tired and more than a little depressed. Our taxi from the airport to our home in Bollington, Macclesfield, seemed to take twice as long as it normally did. We were wholeheartedly convinced by then that Gypsy would not be leaving Koh Samui. I could not wait to be sitting in front of the computer downloading all the emails from the period we were out of the country, in particular the all-important one that Liz Mulqueen had promised to send us. On reaching the house, we dumped the luggage in the porch, stepped over all the mail that had accumulated, and headed upstairs to switch our computer on. Even that seemed to be taking its time, but at last a long list of emails, most of it junk mail, started scrolling up the screen. There was no email at that point, but early next morning I was delighted to see one from Liz.

Welcome home, boys,

it began, and continued with details of a telephone number in Bangkok for us to contact a German lady called Tordis.

She will be able to converse with Brigitte and Werner in their language about Gypsy's travel arrangements. Tordis will meet Gypsy in Bangkok after she has been put on the flight from Koh Samui. She will look after Gypsy in her high-walled garden in the city and she will be safe there. We will have to hope that she doesn't escape again from the DRCS before her plane journey is arranged. I will be in touch when things start moving.

Regards. Liz Mulqueen (Crown Worldwide Handling Agents)

Back Home Again

'What if Gypsy managed to escape from Tordis's walled garden in the centre of Bangkok?'

I successfully filmed the wedding at St. Christopher's Church, Pott Shrigley and Shrigley Hall Hotel on Saturday on automatic pilot, as my mind was filled with the knowledge that at last everything was falling into place like a giant jigsaw puzzle. How I concentrated enough to film it up to my usual standard, I will never know, but I apparently did. With having jet lag, I did actually nod off while the couple were having their wedding breakfast! Thankfully the toastmaster, a friend of mine, woke me up in time to film the speeches! After that episode, I vowed never to book a wedding job so soon after returning from a holiday, especially a long-distance jaunt!

All of a sudden, we felt as though mountains were being moved when messages began arriving from thousands of miles away!

Hello Phil and Bob.

We are pleased to tell you that Gypsy has left Koh Samui now. It is beautiful she did not go with you because I have now got to know Tordis, who is German also. She will help me to get many many dogs homes that are good all over the world and sheep too. (We thought she meant dogs and sheep as well, but read on!) *It will be very very sheep now* (she meant cheap) *to send dogs to Germany, which means there will be more money left for all the sick dogs in the Rescue Centre. This is good! It is something very beautiful you have done Phil and Bob. We are missing you very much already. Please have a big kiss from Brigitte and Werner. Tordis has told me that Gypsy is very well in her new home in Bangkok. This dog loves you very much and you will soon have her in England. God is working in the people's hearts to make this possible.*

Best wishes...Brigitte and Werner: email (DRCS)

*Monday 3pm English time: Gypsy now in Bangkok!
Rescue centre has been more than a bit generous with the tranquilliser, therefore she is more groggy than she should be. She is fine though. She has eaten her first meal since the flight from Koh Samui and tomorrow Tordis will de-tick her. On Wednesday I have to take her to a vet of the Embassy's choosing even though we already have her medical papers. After this, I will take her to get her export license. Hopefully she will travel to England on Thursday on the flight you went on, only a week later. I will keep you informed of our progress here in Bangkok.
Regards Liz Mulqueen: email*

<u>Wednesday – email to Liz and Tordis:</u>
*I know it sounds stupid but I am getting worried now in case the captain forgets there is a dog in the hold. It's a horrible thought that there might be no air-conditioning or temperature control switched on! I can't sleep from thinking about it!
Phil x*

<u>Thursday midday:</u>
*Hello Phil and Bob.
Please don't worry about that. They are fully in the picture. Gypsy now has her export licence and she has had her medical papers renewed by the vet here. She has now left for Bangkok airport for the flight to Heathrow. She will arrive in your country around 7am English time tomorrow. First of all, she will spend around five hours in Bangkok airport so that her papers can be checked, double-checked, and stamped. You know how thorough they have to be. There is no way of avoiding the long wait, but we have sent a handler with her. We have instructed him to walk her on the lead before she finally goes through to the*

under cabin for her eleven-hour flight. He will also feed her a light meal. We have cooked some sausages for her and attached some treats to her cage. She will also be given water to drink before she boards. Please now keep us informed from your end, as she is a beautiful dog, and as you can imagine, we have both become very attached to her. I cried when she left us, but I know she is going to a good home and is much loved by you. We would, of course, like to know in the future how she is adapting to her new life in England from time to time. We have been so pleased to arrange everything to send your lovely dog to you. God bless you both and Gypsy too.

Tordis and Liz: email

Thursday afternoon telephone call:

This is Heathrow Airport. We have a dog called Gypsy arriving on a Thai Airways flight on Friday morning approximately 7:30am. We need confirmation that the quarantine kennels will be here to collect your dog. Can you let us have their telephone number please?

We were overjoyed at this news and could not wait for the week to go by. One thing did worry us, though, with regard to Gypsy's frequent vanishing tricks. What if she managed somehow to escape from Tordis's walled garden in the centre of Bangkok? That would have been an unbearable situation, but all the time we heard nothing, we presumed everything was ok. The following notes, in Thai and English, were fastened to her cage:

PLEASE FEED SAUSAGES IN FOIL TO THE DOG AT 22:00. PLEASE ALSO REFILL THE WATER CONTAINER BEFORE BOARDING. THANK YOU!"

...and...

"PLEASE GIVE ME THESE TREATS ONCE IN A WHILE WHEN PASSING MY KENNEL. THANK YOU!

She was certainly not going to go hungry or thirsty on this amazing trip that so few other dogs had experienced till then. As Gypsy's flight was due to land at Heathrow around 7am-7:30am the following morning, we decided to follow its progress on Teletext. Even this was nail-biting as we discovered that because of air traffic control problems, many flights were circling above the airport in layers, including the Thai Airways flight. We did learn later that her cage had turned upside down during the journey, and because of that she had sustained a limp when she was allowed out of the cage. It was over an hour before the plane was given permission to land, and it was such a relief to know that on landing, she was taken off the plane, exercised briefly, and given a bowl of water. For this service from Heathrow's Animal Care, it cost an astronomical price of £180! To be honest, something of a rip-off, but worth every penny just to finally have her at long last on British soil.

About two hours after our dog had arrived, we received a call from Mike Binks, the owner of the kennels, to advise us that he had collected Gypsy and was now returning with her to Chesterfield. When she arrived at the kennels, we received a lovely phone call from Chris, Mike's partner...

Hello Phil and Bob.

You'll be delighted to hear that I have the most beautiful black dog sitting next to me! She answers to the name of Gypsy...do you know her by any chance? She is up at the house with us now. Oh she is a lovely girl! I cried so much when I met her, thinking about all that she's been through.

What an amazing story. There is no doubt about it, Phil, your prayers have been answered. She is so affectionate and she has taken to us already. She is happy, calm, and contented. Just wait till she sees you walking into the kennels! This will be the best moment in her life!

Gypsy in Quarantine

'We were excited to be at last
taking Gypsy home'

Everything was happily knitting together after so many dramas, so Mike agreed to letting us visit the kennels the following day. He explained that we should not expect too much from Gypsy, as she could still be disorientated and probably still be feeling the effects of the pre-flight tranquilliser and medication. We set off early the following morning on a series of three connecting buses, as we did not own a car. These took us through the Peak District, which included Buxton and a number of picturesque villages, till we eventually arrived at Chesterfield, a very quaint market town. From there we had to catch a local service to Caitlow, where the kennels were situated, but a problem suddenly arose. The bus driver did not know where we had to leave the bus, as Deepsick Lane, where the kennels were, was not on the bus route.

We briefly explained the purpose of our long trek to Chesterfield, and he looked incredulous! He pulled up near this very grand detached residence and said he would wait while I knocked on the front door. We left the bus, walked down the drive, and knocked loudly, and after a few minutes' conversation with a lady, we were called over by the house owner. He very kindly offered to drive us to Calagran as he knew where it was, so we climbed into his Bentley and arrived in style after thanking the bus driver! We were truly overwhelmed by the actions of the bus driver and now this gentleman. It is surprising how kindness rises to the surface, particularly when related to animals. We got the impression that the bus passengers were behind us all the way too. It is not often one hears something like the tale we had to tell, and I must say we had a captive audience hanging onto every word! I don't think they minded their journeys being delayed a little.

One elderly lady called Martha gave me her telephone number, as she wanted to know how everything went. We became quite friendly over the next few months, and we even met her twice in Chesterfield. On one occasion she went with us to see Gypsy as she desperately wanted to meet her, and we kept in touch for many years, mostly by email. Quite often we travelled on the bus with the same driver who initially helped us on our first visit, so he was also kept up to date. Because it was off the beaten track, we still had a fair walk to the kennels but became used to it, regardless of the weather.

As we nervously approached the gate with butterflies in our stomachs, we felt so strange. We guessed what Gypsy's reaction would be when she realised we were there. Our main concern was that she had recovered from what must have been an unsettling series of events for an animal. To put it mildly, when Gypsy saw us coming towards her kennel, she was ecstatically excited and leapt up and down, barking and wagging her tail furiously. It was wonderful to now know that everything we'd been through had been worthwhile. We spent about ninety minutes with her, and it was a real wrench having to leave her so soon to return home. Mike's partner, Chris said that Gypsy was always considerably upset after we'd gone, so she sat with her for a while. Apparently, many times after we left her, she tore up her bedding with sheer frustration, and it had to be replaced over and over again.

On each visit via Buxton, we called into a pet shop and bought her huge, meaty bones and other treats. Some weeks later I said to Chris, Gypsy's kennel is just like a boneyard, but she said to leave them with her as they were her 'belongings'! The only thing we were worried about was this limp that Gypsy had, so a visit to the vet was arranged.

He x-rayed it and said she must have had a fracture some time back, and being jostled about in the plane hold had probably strained it. It soon cleared up, thankfully, but it added more expense to our ever-increasing debt!

On our second visit a few days later, the temperature had dropped considerably for the time of year, and even though it was only mid-May, Chris installed a heater in Gypsy's boudoir. All the time our dog was with Calagran, she gave her special attention by sitting with her for long periods or taking her to their house sometimes. Our journeys over to Chesterfield were fraught at times with delays, missed connections, and quite often because of bad weather. That six months seemed as though it was destined to never end, but we made it more enjoyable by stopping off at different country pubs when possible. We got to know Derbyshire extremely well and occasionally continued to visit some of those places.

As Gypsy had to be quarantined for a period of six months, we estimated that visiting her twice a week would mean that we had approximately around fifty return trips to do! A possible total of around one hundred and fifty buses! On a couple of rare occasions, friends of ours drove us over to see her, so that was bliss and very helpful! Within a few weeks, though, Chris began driving us into the centre of Chesterfield, which made things a little easier. It also gave us the opportunity to have a coffee or a glass of wine with her before starting our long journey back home.

On one of our visits to the kennels, we were introduced to a lady called Marjorie whose sister had two kittens that were being boarded there. She was living abroad, so I was asked if I could make a short film of them to send to her in France, as Chris had let her know that I was a professional cameraman. I gladly agreed to do so, and I earned a fee for producing it, which of course helped towards our travel expenses.

Bob's email to Brigitte...

We hope you and Werner are keeping well. I thought we had better update you on Gypsy's progress on this side of the world. She is happily settled in at the boarding kennels even though she gets so agitated when we leave her each time. We still cannot imagine how she must have felt going through all those airport procedures. It was bad enough for us, as you know what Bangkok airport is like. Its vast, sprawling area is like being part of a massive ant colony when checking in and traversing the airport. Every time we have experienced it, we have always been on edge praying we are not going to miss the flight because of the long queues.

Thank you so much for inviting us over to Berlin in December when you go there to see your parents. Hopefully we can do this, as it is somewhere we have not been before. If we do, it will probably be over the New Year period for a few days. It will be strange seeing you both outside of the hot climate in Koh Samui, wearing winter woollies!!

We are counting the weeks to when Gypsy can say goodbye to the kennels in November, as it's getting very tiring and hectic travelling back and forth all the time. That will be fun when all the dogs get together for the first time! I will take some photos and email them to you.

Love to you both and all the dogs and cats you are caring for.

Bob and Phil. xxxx

As the summer went by, Gypsy's coat gradually grew thicker, and when cold November came, she was well insulated against the impending winter weather. It was considerably sad as well as exciting when we went to the kennels for the last time. We were excited to be at last taking Gypsy home, yet we had grown very fond of Chris and Mike, who were upset to see Gypsy go, as they had become so very attached to her. Chris drove us all into Chesterfield to catch our first bus, and Gypsy seemed to enjoy the journey. We had a departing drink in a wine bar we had previously been to with Chris before saying goodbye. We had a short time in between the different buses, so we were able to exercise her, but during the journey between Buxton and Macclesfield, Gypsy was physically sick due to the steep and ever-winding roads.

En route we passed the Cat and Fiddle, reportedly the highest pub in England, though some might dispute that. After several years of being closed, it was recently revamped and has now become a whisky distillery. This was a regular watering hole for bikers, and the area was notorious for biking accidents, as the roads are mostly hairpin bends. We would sometimes take the dogs there during the summer months, where they could run quite freely on the hills.

The final leg of the trip was in a taxi from Macclesfield to Bollington and the slightly dreaded 'canine summit meeting!' As you can imagine, there was much growling, particularly from the ones we already had, which was three at the time. After about a week or so, they gradually became acclimatised to each other, and Gypsy integrated very well and actually became the boss!

Phil's email to Brigitte & Werner...

We just wanted you to know that Gypsy is happily enjoying living with us and our other dogs. Not too many problems integrating them, and Gypsy is actually 'in charge!' We cannot thank you enough for all you did financially to enable us to get her to England and for homing her at the clinic, knowing she was causing you so much stress! We will soon begin to pay some money into your account. What a surprise when we arrived home to read your latest newsletter and see a photo of Rhino and one of us with him. Such a cute little thing whom we hope will get much better. We will continue to sponsor him until that time comes. Maybe we will be able to bring him over here to join the ever-growing canine family sometime?

Fetching Gypsy to England was a highly traumatic experience for all of us, but through our determination and your cooperation, everything has fallen into place. We will, of course, be returning to Koh Samui again, probably next year, to help out at the rescue centre, as it is the least we can do. Gypsy will have her holiday in the kennels with our other dogs. You will always be in our hearts, no matter how great the distance is between us. God bless you both and all the animals in your care. We will keep you informed about Gypsy's life over here, which will be full of adventures, I am sure.

With much love from Phil and Bob xxxx

Artistic me in the DRCS

Feeding a starving dog

A rather concerned Brigitte

Werner and I feeling despondent

```
***********************
***   TX REPORT    ***
***********************

TRANSMISSION OK

TX/RX NO              2037
CONNECTION TEL              9006622499036
SUBADDRESS
CONNECTION ID
ST. TIME              06/05 10:31
USAGE T               03'37
PGS.                  2 ( 5)
RESULT                OK
```

TO LIZ at CROWN WORLD WIDE - BANGKOK
Fax 00 66 2 249 9036

03-05-2000 10:05   FROM CALAGRAN KENNELS   TO 1363006677422412   P.01

Calagran Quarantine Kennels

Quarantine Kennels & Carrying Agents. Authorised by the Ministry of Agriculture

DEEPSICK LANE
Nr. CALOW
CHESTERFIELD
DERBYSHIRE S44 5DN
ENGLAND

FAX MESSAGE

Date:
To: ROBERT COOPER   Date: 3-5-00   From: Tel. No: (44) 1246 211281
Room 3102   Fax No: (44) 1246 231039

* PLEASE CALL WHEN RECEIVED (MR. COOPER) *
GYPSY'S IMPORT LICENCE FOLLOWS THIS (NO 0/0034299)
PLUS RED PASSPORT IMPORT LABEL (NOW GREEN!)
I CONFIRM THAT I WILL MEET GYPSY AT
MANCHESTER OFF THE BK/035 on 5 MAY
PLEASE ADVISE ME OF THE AIR WAY BILL NUMBER WHEN
YOU HAVE BOOKED HER
       Best Wishes   Kite R   MIKE BINKS

DATE TO

Note to Liz from Calagran Boarding Kennels

Ministry of Agriculture, Fisheries and Food
Animal Health (Disease Control) Division, Branch A,
1A, Page Street, London, SW1P 4PQ
Telephone No. 020 7904 6222 Fax: 020 7904 6013

Reference	
IDY	0/0034299

Animal Health Act 1981
The Rabies (Importation of Dogs, Cats and Other Mammals) Order 1974 (as amended)
The Pet Travel Scheme (Pilot Arrangements) (England) Order 1999

Release of dog(s) /cats(s) from quarantine

The animal(s) listed below may not be released from the quarantine premises until the date shown below, upon which date the detention and isolation period will expire, unless prior authority is given for the animals transfer to another quarantine premises or port or airport for export.

Description of animal(s)	DOG - LABRADOR CROSS 1 OF
Name of owner	MR R. COOPER
Authorised place of detention	CALAGRAN QUARANTINE KENNELS NR CALOW CHESTERFIELD DERBYSHIRE S44 5DN
Date of landing	12/05/2000
Date of release	11/11/2000

Signature: *[signature]* (for the Minister of Agriculture, Fisheries and Food)   Date: 03 October 2000

Name in BLOCK LETTERS: MR D. BAKRANIA

ID 55 (Rev. 2/00)

Quarantine form

Ulrike speaking to Brigitte about Gypsy

With friends from the Baan Samui Hotel

Phil cooling off on Chaweng beach

With a post-op puppy

Time for my new image!

Gypsy in her English bed

Gypsy at home in Bollington

Gypsy and Gretel on the slopes of White Nancy, Bollington

Travelling in style to Liverpool

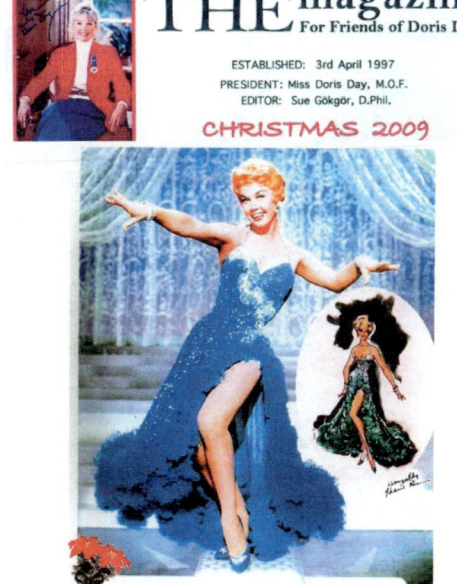

I wrote for this Magazine for 4 years

Peter and I at Paradise Park

The unique pastel shaded free flying doves

Phil with Peter at Paradise Park

Talkative parrot at Paradise Park

From here to infinity pool!

Phi Phi island boat trip

Maya beach near Phi Phi Island on last Thai Holiday

With another monkey friend on Phi Phi Island

Six years on from 2004 tsunami

Toby... the last dog in my life

St.George's Day, Cotton Tree with best friend Bev

Christina and Jayne, Cotton Tree

The Poachers quiz night in aid of the DRCS

Living in Bollington

'I don't think many folk have had their dogs
spending a night behind bars'

Initially, taking Gypsy out for walks was slightly problematic, as she was so used to running around most of the time minus a lead in Koh Samui. Trying to give her more freedom in the hills of Bollington, we removed her lead, and she would run to the top of a slope, wait for us to approach within a few feet, then she would run off again. This game she played became very exhausting, and on one occasion she just disappeared completely as dusk was falling. It began to rain heavily, and as it grew darker, we thought that after all we had achieved bringing her to England, there was now a chance that she could become lost and we may never find her again.

Phil and I split up and wandered around the fields for nearly three hours until eventually I heard a whimpering inside some bushes. When I called her name, there was a rustling and she appeared very sheepishly with her head down. Very relieved to find her, I took her home and vowed to always keep her on a lead from then on. Our garden was large enough for the dogs to freely exercise, though, so there was no problem there.

One afternoon, Gypsy accidentally escaped out by the back gate on her own. On the farm nearby we heard loud squealing noises, and we found her chasing two pigs (Pinky and Perky we called them) around a very muddy field and the very irate farmer turning the air blue!! I had to climb over a stone wall and squelch through all that mire until I caught her! Thankfully that was a one-off experience! On another occasion, Gypsy managed to push the back gate latch up with her nose, and next moment all of our dogs were running loose around the Bollington countryside! After much calling, Gypsy and Heidi returned soon after, but Bruno and Toby remained somewhere out in the darkness.

We were out of our minds with worry and went out with torches in an attempt to find them, but unfortunately, we had no luck. Arriving dejectedly back at our house, we found a message had been left on our answerphone asking us to call Macclesfield Police Station urgently. We did so and were told, "Hello sir, I think we have a couple of dogs here that belong to you." We were staggered to hear this but so overjoyed, and we asked the sergeant how on earth that had happened. Apparently, someone driving down a lane in nearby Pott Shrigley spotted our two dogs running freely around midnight and realised they were probably lost, so they took them into the police station for safekeeping. Fortunately, both dogs had a medallion on their collars containing our phone number, so they were able to contact us. As it was very late, they agreed to keep them in a spare cell till the next morning. I don't think many folk have had their dogs spending a night behind bars! All down to Gypsy, of course!

One day, whilst I was signing for a parcel delivered by the postman, Gypsy sneakily pushed past him and scarpered down the street like a rocket. I ran after her and saw her going through the gates of St. John's Church in nearby Church Street. Making sure there were no open graves, I chased her all round the cemetery, but she then went back through the gates and ran towards the village. I was becoming more out of breath and slowed down, so briefly I lost sight of her. Passing Heathcote's Butchers, Jeremy was standing in the doorway, so I asked if he had seen Gypsy. His reply was, "Yes, on the other side of the road, going like the clappers. She's probably on her way back to Thailand, ha ha!" Being so stressed out, his sense of humour was lost on me at that moment. I caught sight of her about a hundred yards ahead and gradually caught her up after getting someone to stop her. I then realised I had no lead with me so I had to carry her back to the house in my arms and suddenly I became aware that I had run right through the village in my carpet slippers! I felt quite embarrassed by that, but the main thing was that I had managed to catch her.

After Gypsy had settled in over the winter months, we decided we should visit some relatives and introduce Gypsy officially to them. One such day we arranged to go to Liverpool, where Phil's sister Gill lived in Crosby and where he was brought up as a child. We set off by train from Macclesfield heading for Manchester when suddenly Gypsy, ever friendly, decided to leap onto this fellow's lap and lick his face! You can imagine his reaction, as it was not at all welcome. We apologised profusely for this and explained the reason she was on this train.

Well, this opened the floodgates as all the surrounding passengers homed in on our story about her leaving Thailand, and it became a sort of 'An Audience with Bob and Phil'. They were fascinated to hear as much as possible, and that journey on to Liverpool became the most interesting train ride ever for us and the other people. At one point a seat became available by the window, and for a short while our dog sat quietly there watching the world glide by, totally unperturbed. In due course the ticket inspector informed us that she had to sit under the table, so we had to abide by that. Gill thought it was hilarious when we arrived, and I am pleased to say we did a few more trips with Gypsy which were quite uneventful, even taking her to Burnley, where Phil's father lived. Unfortunately, his wife did not appreciate dogs, so it was quite uncomfortable at times!

Since Gypsy has lived in England, we have returned to Koh Samui on three more occasions. The first time, our fourth visit, was very strange. Everywhere we went, we expected to see Gypsy there, because we had been to so many places with her. We felt guilty to be enjoying the beach, the sea, and the tropical weather while she was spending her 'vacation' in Studholme Boarding Kennels in Wilmslow with our other dogs. Of course we were with Brigitte and Werner much of the time, socially and also doing some work at the Dog Rescue Centre. We also made friends with the volunteer helpers that came from various countries around the world, who spent a considerable part of their holidays helping the dogs and cats at the DRCS, like we did.

One of our trips to Koh Samui was highly unusual, to say the least. We chose to fly with Finnair, which meant staying for one night in Helsinki. The temperature was minus 20 degrees Fahrenheit, and the city was under several feet of snow. The ships in the harbour were embedded in ice at least one foot thick, like decorations set on a Christmas cake. We enjoyed sampling the local herrings and beer despite feeling frozen to the bone. The sauna at our hotel was very much appreciated afterwards.

The following day we caught our next flight, which called in at a small Swedish airport called Kiruna, where we disembarked, checked in, and reboarded before the long, unbroken flight to Bangkok. We had decided to spend one night in Bangkok (cue for a song there!) so we were taken by taxi to the Marriot Hotel on the Chao Phraya River. At 2am we were languishing in a steamy jacuzzi in 33 degrees under some tall palm trees knocking back a Mekong or two and the odd cocktail! Next morning we travelled along the river on a small boat moored outside our hotel to a street market for lunch. What we had done so far was amazing, yet we had not even begun our main holiday. During the afternoon we once again took that short flight to our dream destination.

In 2002 we had decided on this occasion to have a two-centre holiday with ten days in the Chaweng Regent hotel and then eight days in Bophut further round the island. The former consisted mostly of bungalows positioned around an infinity pool. We spent several occasions sitting on our veranda with our next-door neighbour, an attractive young woman called Vivienne, but sometimes it became a bit wearing! She seemed to have an axe to grind over everything and was continually putting the world to rights, and our ideas and opinions seemed insignificant to her. The hotel itself we could not fault, and we enjoyed the occasional barbecues on the beachfront.

On the tenth day we were more than ready to move on to our next hotel, which was a much smaller and compact establishment called Eden Bungalows, situated in Bophut. There were only six bungalows situated around a small pool within beautifully kept gardens. The owners, Gerard and Lydia, were from France and owned a dog which we became very fond of. While we were resident there, we arranged for Brigitte and Werner to have a social evening with us and the owners. It went really well as they got to know each other, after which Lydia agreed to place a donation box and leaflets in the reception area, which we were thrilled about. Despite being encouraged by Brigitte to have their dog Max vaccinated, they failed to do so and he sadly died soon afterwards.

Speaking of which, Brigitte asked us if we were confident enough to approach some hotels with a view to persuading them to help the DRCS by doing something similar. Of course we said we would, so she gave us a list of four hotels. Two in Chaweng and two in another resort further around the coast called Maenam. So that we appeared legitimate and official, she gave us both a green and yellow t-shirt, each with their logo very prominent. We also had a supply of leaflets and small donation boxes. It was not easy convincing them to accept them, but once we hinted that they might end up on the DRCS list of non-dog-friendly hotels, it helped to sway three of them. Unfortunately, we were unsuccessful with one in Maenam, so they became a new inclusion on the banned list! They could not remove us from the premises quick enough! Brigitte was very pleased with the main result and said we should extend our holidays or go more often!

On this holiday, Phil was celebrating his 50th birthday, so we decided to do something unusual. The other waterfall was called Na Muang 2 and was quite inaccessible and only reached by scaling up a very steep slope on highly precarious rocky steps. In hindsight we should not have thought we were as capable as Sir Edmund Hillary and Sherpa Tensing reaching the summit of Mount Everest! It became more and more difficult, and about halfway up we decided enough was enough. We reluctantly gave in and started our descent, which was almost as difficult as getting to that stage.

During this climb downwards, Phil fell backwards and banged his head on a thick branch and sustained a huge lump. Of course I got the blame, as it was me that suggested this special day out. By now we had realised that it had been a huge mistake trying to be so adventurous, and eventually we reached ground level. A short walk from there led us into a tiny village with a bar and, luckily, a small chemist. From there we were able to get a taxi back to our hotel. Never did anywhere look so birthday friendly, so we ensconced ourselves in their beach bar for the remainder of the day!

Each time we returned to Thailand, we were given the inevitable 'advice' not to bring another dog back to England; why I will never know! We had no intention of doing that, but it does not mean we weren't tempted. It was so easy to become attached to any of the suffering dogs in the centre, and in 2004 there was one in particular that Phil became besotted with. He was a small, long-eared breed, but unfortunately, he was completely bald with a pot belly. His skin felt and looked like grey parchment, so we nicknamed him Rhino. With him having treatment, there was no question of him leaving Thailand, so after much consideration, we decided to sponsor his upkeep. Depending on his progress, we contemplated the possibility of bringing him to Bollington at a suitable time in the future. This was not to be, unfortunately, as we were sadly notified three months later that poor Rhino's health had deteriorated so much he had been put to sleep. Such a tragic end to this adorable little creature, and we were naturally heartbroken at this news.

During this holiday, one innovation we discovered was the introduction of webcams positioned near selected hotels. On Lamai beach, a resort further round the coast, we discovered they had placed one in a hotel over the beach the previous year. At this particular time we were unaware of something similar in Chaweng, but it was fascinating to discover that we could watch the holiday resort from thousands of miles away. It so happened when we stayed in the Samui Nation a few years after bringing Gypsy to England, we were able to log on at a certain time and see the friends we had made enjoying themselves. Occasionally we would see the odd stray dog wandering by along the beach. Of course it also gave us pangs of envy as we looked out of the window at home, staring at heavy rain showers or snow-covered fields.

One of the most upsetting times we had when working at the dog centre was when we were attempting to cover about forty dogs with tick powder in very humid temperatures. It was all just a game to them as they dodged us as much as they could and we became more and more exhausted. Sometimes, there seemed to be more powder on us than the dogs! The worst part of this exercise was when we attempted to remove the ticks from some of the more infected dogs with tweezers. It was nigh impossible as they were so riddled with them and writhing so much with the pain. One little dog died squealing in agony on Phil's lap, and it was heart-wrenching witnessing the last moments of this poor animal's life.

Eliminating ticks was a major problem, and despite the dogs being powdered regularly and injected with Ivomec, some ticks managed to resist this treatment. Wit, the manager, suggested buying a flamethrower, usually used for burning bristles off slaughtered pigs, so Rid was given the job of using this to burn the ticks away that lived inside the walls. Not off the dogs' coats as well, I must point out!

Something that used to amuse us was the fact that most names, particularly among the male community, were only three letters long. Names like Wit, Rid, Egg, Keo, Tom, Bin, and Don, to name a few. Being called Bob, I fitted in very nicely! There was one worker with a four-letter word, unfortunately called 'Dung'! I don't think he was aware of the connotation! Oh, and of course we have to mention 'Pong'! I don't believe for one moment that they were related!

On this holiday in 2004 we were staying in the Chaba Cabana Hotel at the northernmost tip of Chaweng beach. A more beautiful, idyllic stretch of sand you could not wish to find. We were considered by several of the guests to be rather eccentric, choosing to spend many days working at the dog centre instead of lazing by the pool like they were doing every day. We used to return to the hotel early evening, covered in perspiration and tick powder, just as everyone was heading out for a night in the town in their finest clothes!! When they discovered the real reason we were in that condition, they were quite sympathetic, and some of them even helped by making donations. We were not able to entice them to work with us at the centre, though! It was difficult at times trying to erase those tragic moments we encountered from our minds and enjoy the better things Koh Samui had to offer.

Just around the corner from our hotel on a small stretch of sand was a boutique hotel called Le Papillon (Butterfly). In a way we wished we had known about it first, and we often rounded off our evenings in there with our Aussie friends. It would have been considerably less expensive. Some guests staying there recommended another hotel and restaurant to us, in the sleepy village of Thong Krut called 'Hemingways on the Bay.' We just had to arrange a visit, so we hired a minibus one evening, and what a memorable night that was.

It was situated in the south of the island and had unbelievable views of the nearby small islands of Koh Tan and Koh Mudsum. They offered short speedboat trips to both of them, and sometimes they organised similar trips on long boats. It goes without saying that the cuisine was out of this world, though highly expensive, but worth hiring a taxi for, which a group of us did from our hotel.

One of the most memorable nights we ever had out of many, and my mouth waters at the thought of that exceptional range of exotic dishes!

At the end of this holiday we were given a parting gift from Brigitte. It was a book written by His Majesty, King of Thailand, Bhumibol Adulyade, and was called 'The Story of Tongdaeng: Biography of a Pet Dog.' She inscribed it, 'To my English friends Bob and Phil, with love,' and we were so touched by this gesture, considering it was so rare and precious. The King wrote this account of his dog in Thai, which was translated into English and was lavishly illustrated.

Also before we left, we were introduced to a young American lady called Belinda, an artist who was fascinated to hear Gypsy's story. As the new dog compound had been recently opened in Ban Taling Nam, Brigitte asked her to paint Gypsy's portrait on the main wall, which was done from a photo we gave her. Unfortunately, this painting was completed just after we flew back to the UK, so we only saw the finished work on our next trip in 2007. By then, though, the sun and constant heat had faded it considerably, which we felt sad about.

We were well aware of the problems Brigitte faced with some staff, and she had a unique way of dealing with them. One such person who shall be nameless left very suddenly, and she was the last to know, but this was a common occurrence. The guy owed Brigitte sixty euros, so she had 'agreed' on an earlier occasion with her Thai staff that she would spread the cost amongst the remaining colleagues if that ever happened! This arrangement was not very well received, as you can imagine, but it worked, and it usually made them spill the beans about any impending departure if they were aware of it! The staff generally never gave any notice of leaving but just did not turn up to work without any explanations! A Thai trait apparently!

Tsunami!

'The only news they had, was that they were missing presumed dead'

At the end of 2004, a week before Christmas, we had a call from Donna and Graham, who we had been friends with since meeting them in the Baan Samui hotel on our second stay there. They lived in Carlisle, Cumbria, with their five-year-old daughter, Cindy. They had decided to book a last-minute holiday to Thailand again for two weeks over the holiday season and this time chose Phuket for a change. Of course we were excited for them and wished them all the best. They made tentative arrangements to come and see us in Bollington again during February after they arrived home, which of course we were looking forward to.

On Boxing Day, the awful news of a tsunami in the South China Sea was announced on TV. Immediately we thought of our friends in Phuket, which seemed to be one of the islands most severely affected. We were glued to each news bulletin, praying that they were not among the victims who had drowned. I tried texting and calling Donna's mobile phone, but there was no response, so naturally we became very concerned. Next, we sent an email, but that remained unanswered, so we could only hope they would contact us at some point.

A few more days went by with still no news, and by then we realised that by now they should have returned home. Graham had his own haulage business, so in desperation I telephoned the company. The secretary said that she was sorry to tell me that the only news she had was that they were listed as 'missing presumed dead'. The more we recalled seeing the devastating TV footage of the mammoth waves destroying everything in their path, the more horrified we became. On several islands and along the coast, many of the popular resorts were wiped out. Koh Samui was only slightly damaged, and it was heartbreaking to think that our friends booked somewhere different at the last minute. Fate can deal a cruel hand sometimes.

We had such fond memories of this lovely family, especially our evenings sitting near the water's edge outside the Jah Dub till the early hours. They were staying in a room only yards away, so they kept popping in and out to check on Cindy. Donna was a self-confessed shopaholic, and on a couple of evenings we spent time visiting the local market stalls and shops. As they were about to move into a new property in England, Donna just had to have some items from Thailand. She was in a master class when haggling over the prices and one time she settled on a giant table lamp, a huge vase, and a couple of pictures. This was apart from the numerous dresses she bought! Each time she made a purchase, Graham's eyes ascended into heaven, and he became more agitated. "How on earth are we going to get all of these through customs?" he enquired anxiously. Unperturbed by that question, Donna replied, "We'll just have to pay the excess baggage charges, hun!" which concerned Graham even more. I could not imagine the pandemonium they must have caused when they were checking in at the airport! Sadly we never did find out exactly what happened to them, but we fear the worst, as we never heard from them again.

Phil had only been reunited with his birth mother in 2005, so we decided to stay with his family in Pevensey, Eastbourne, for a few days. We were then going to fly from Heathrow on what would be our final trip to Koh Samui in 2007, so his mother and sister Wendy drove us to the station to catch our train. As you can imagine, it was quite an emotional goodbye as we watched the car drive off, then suddenly, like a ton of bricks, something very important hit me. "Phil! Our cases!" I yelled, as they were still in the boot!

By now their car was about 150 yards away and heading rapidly towards some traffic lights. We furiously waved our arms and shouted our heads off, and fortunately the lights turned to red, which gave them longer to see us. We did not have Wendy's mobile phone number, so we could not contact them that way. They crossed through the lights on green and we still weren't sure if they had noticed us till we saw them returning in our direction. What a sense of relief we had as we barely had five minutes left to unload the cases from the boot and drag them onto the platform. This was the only train that connected with our flight, so once in a while miracles do happen!

Prior to this holiday, Phil had been suffering several bouts of angina, so we decided that he would need wheelchair assistance, particularly in Bangkok's supersized airport, which, to give its full name, is called Suvarnabhumi. When we landed, he was designated a wheelchair and a young member of airport staff to push him along the lengthy corridors. I could barely keep up with him considering the speed the attendant was walking. As this was 2am in the morning, we were taken to a small, comfortable lounge for a few hours till our ongoing flight at 7am. This meant we were able to 'sleep' on some long cushioned seats. We were collected from there at 6am to check in and spent half an hour in the Royal Orchid hospitality lounge before boarding. Tea, coffee, soft drinks, savoury snacks, and cakes were served there completely free of charge. The care and attention we received throughout was unbelievable.

On reaching Koh Samui we were deposited in the airport's V.I.P. lounge along with six Buddhist monks to await our coach transfer. What amazing men they were, with a few of them speaking English extremely well. They could not believe it when we related our story of Gypsy's adventures. Our choice of hotel this time was the Samui Natien, which is where we originally met Gypsy for the first time eight years earlier. It was idyllic having a bungalow on the beach itself. Dogs often wandered past, and in particular one Alsatian started sleeping on our veranda. Before Phil could broach the subject, I said, "Please don't get any ideas, Phil! We don't want history repeating itself! Besides, he is wearing a collar, so we couldn't even consider whisking him away!" That was just as well, I think, as we became very attached to that dog, which we called Sammy while we were there. He only randomly stayed outside our bungalow, so we did not have the trauma of saying goodbye to him on the last night.

Whilst back on the island, we of course still wanted to explore places we had not yet visited. One such place was the Paradise Park Farm on the island's highest mountain, which had only been opened since we were last there. This should be a major attraction on everyone's itinerary. It is in the same area as the DRCS and spans twenty acres, so one day we combined both places. In the morning we helped out with the dogs, then in the afternoon, paid our first visit to the park. It is positioned at the highest point in Koh Samui, where you can view the whole island and surrounding islands too. The perfect vantage point was whilst languishing in the infinity pool, so that took up an hour approximately!

On arrival into the reception area, there was a turquoise and yellow parrot that loved to sit on people's shoulders. It was quite talkative, but some of the expressions were not quite what we expected. It seemed to have a favourite one of 'bugger off', which some wicked person had taught it. 'Have a nice day' was a better and more sociable one! We heard it once say both together, which was so funny, and I just wish I could have recorded that moment!

There are so many facets to the park you need at least a couple of visits to appreciate everything it has to offer. In particular, it was thrilling for us to see a vast number of wild deer roaming around in a compound, and visitors were allowed to feed them. It was also fascinating to watch the famous 'free flying painted doves' in a range of pastel colours. A huge variety of animal and bird life can be observed, like rabbits, horses, cows, pygmy goats, ponies, peacocks, and ducks. There was even an emu strutting around.

Positioned throughout the grounds were small rivers and waterfalls, and it truly lives up to the name of Paradise. Obviously, there was also a wide range of places to eat: coffee bars, snack bars, poolside bar, and a very reputable restaurant high in its placement but not in its prices. All of these are set in the most magnificent garden areas full of orchids and other exotic flowers, plants and trees. One can also unwind in the spa, and the phrase 'heaven on earth' springs to mind. Unfortunately, there was no accommodation on site there, but nearby you could find places to stay.

One amusing event involved a resident monkey which was called Peter even though it was female. For some reason it became immensely attracted to Phil. She clung to him the whole time and allowed him to walk her round the complex on a lead. In other words, she had adopted him! When it was time to leave, Phil was told in reception, "Peter loves you!" They suggested we could take her back to our hotel and fetch her back the following day! Instantaneously Phil was enthusiastic about this unusual opportunity to own a pet monkey for a day without considering the possible consequences! Being the practical one, I pointed the following pitfalls out to him:

1) What if it escapes from the hotel?
2) What if it does damage?
3) What if it attacks someone?

Phil fully understood what I was saying and reluctantly handed her over to the handler. Peter did not want to be parted from Phil, and there was much clinging and screeching taking place... from the monkey as well! Eventually we were able to leave but must admit it was very upsetting, especially for our furry friend. We managed to steer clear of Peter on the second visit for obvious reasons, as we did not want a repeat performance of the situation.

Two years later we paid a visit to Koh Phi Phi, which was severely damaged in that tsunami, and the island's infrastructure was gradually rebuilt. It meant that there were no roads as such, so most people cycled about, and handcarts were pushed around the narrow streets to deliver goods to the shops and restaurants. It was like going back to a previous era, which we rather liked. It was a pleasant change staying on another island too. We had to fly to Krabi from Bangkok, then catch a high-speed motor launch to Koh Phi Phi. What an exhilarating journey that was, being tossed around the boat and nearly going overboard several times! One of our cases almost disappeared over the side! My back pain was exacerbated for a few days after that. We could have gone more sedately on a passenger boat, but that took over two hours, sailing only twice a day, and we had missed both of those anyway.

Needless to say, the prospect of the return journey in two weeks in the same way perturbed us, but it was less rough then, I am glad to say.

We enjoyed several boat trips around the island to places like Monkey Beach. What a bunch of thieves those animals were, snatching food and drinks from anyone they could get near to, and we became quite scared of them. We had to, of course, visit Maya Bay, which was featured considerably in the Leonardo DiCaprio film 'The Beach.' Strangely enough, Koh Samui was not even mentioned in the film despite it being in the book! Sadly, due to the increase in tourism after the film was released, it became too overcrowded and appeared worse for wear when we arrived there. With so many boats moored there, there was barely room to even paddle! Some years later I read that it was being closed for six months out of each year to regenerate and keep in good condition.

Another trip incorporated Shark Bay, but when we were encouraged to jump into the sea off the boat, I never realised it was in the middle of a group of basking baby sharks! After two minutes I saw them swimming around about twenty feet below me. Although probably quite tame, I could not wait to get back on board. Phil kept calling me to return to the boat, but the tide kept pushing me away, which made me have to swim faster to catch it. I was so exhausted, but what a relief that was to be out of the water. That last trip to Thailand was so memorable in many ways.

Friends of Doris Day

'With much love and kind wishes,
Doris Day'

Gypsy adapted so well to living in Bollington, and it was hilarious seeing her reaction to snow during her first winter in England. She seemed to enjoy rolling over in it and charging into small snow drifts with the other dogs, Hero, Adam and Heidi. In retrospect, a few months after Gypsy first arrived in England, Brigitte emailed us and said...

> *The best thing that's happened to this Dog Rescue Centre, is you meeting Gypsy and us meeting you! At least sixty more dogs have left the island to live in Europe, mostly Germany, with Liz and Tordis being able to arrange everything. We are looking forward so much to when you next come over, which is hopefully next year. Please don't bring Gypsy with you though, ha ha! Thank you so much. All our love. xxx.*

Of course that figure has vastly increased in the years since, so Gypsy, in effect, is the 'patron saint of rehomed dogs!' By bringing one dog to the UK, we never realised what it would lead to and feel very proud that we unintentionally achieved better lives for so many more.

All my life I have been a Doris Day fan, and in the summer of 2007, I started subscribing to the magazine Friends of Doris Day. This was devoted to all aspects of Doris's film and music career, plus a great emphasis on all her work with animal welfare, particularly dogs. In passing, I mentioned Gypsy to the editor Sue Gokgor, and she persuaded me to tell her the full story. I agreed to serialise it over three issues unpaid, of course, starting with the summer 2008 edition. The whole story was condensed into approximately six A4 sheets with photos. I subsequently wrote a further article called Gypsy Ten Years On in 2010.

The response was amazing from all around the world, and here is a selection of a few of those heartfelt and encouraging comments...

Dear Bob....I so enjoyed reading your heart warming story about Gypsy as did my friends and neighbours here in Carmel. We all wish you a long and happy life with her in England. With much love and kind wishes.
DORIS DAY xxx

I loved reading everyone's contributions specially Bob's... please oh please let there be a happy ending to Gypsy's story.
ANNIE (UK)

My favourite story is about Gypsy. I was so touched by her loyalty to Bob and his friend Phil. I hope it is a happy ending and I can't wait for the next magazine to read what happens next.
SHIRLEY SEPULVEDA (USA)

As for the 'Pet Talk' section, I read Bob Cooper's story about Gypsy out loud to my husband Kevin one evening and we were both practically in tears. We are both on the edge of our seats waiting to read part two.
JOANNE MASSEY (UK)

I thoroughly enjoyed reading Bob's account of Gypsy. Roll on when we find out what eventually happened. I just pray that it ends well.
ALFIE RUSSELL (AUSTRALIA)

I thought the 'Pet Talk' page was lovely with the story about Gypsy and Bob. I hope there will be a happy outcome.
ROY FURNIVAL (UK)

I was very moved by Bob Cooper's story about Gypsy. I hope and pray that this ends happily. I cannot wait for the next instalment to find out.
FRANCOISE (FRANCE)

I really hope that the amazing story about Gypsy has a happy ending. She deserves it and so do they!
SHEILA GRAVES (UK).

I particularly liked Bob and Gypsy's story. I just pray that everything will end happily. She is such a beautiful dog and I'm sure Bob will give her a wonderful home.
PAUL O'BRIEN (UK)

Fingers crossed Gypsy's story reaches a happy conclusion in the next issue (boy you do believe in cliff hangers don't you Sue!)
ANTOINETTE FERGUSON (USA)

I also loved Gypsy's story. It just goes to show that the love of an animal can bring about circumstances you could never ever dream of. I would have done exactly the same.
VELDA LULIC (CANADA)

What an amazing experience for you both and especially for Gypsy. I wonder what was going through her mind on her journey to England? It doesn't bear thinking about!
MALCOLM PETERSON (DUBLIN)

I have to admit that Gypsy's story was the first piece I turned to. Many of you might think what a lucky doggie she is. Even though I agree with you, I also think that Bob and Phil were so lucky to find her in the first place. The hours of joy she has brought them will be worth all the stress they had getting her to England. What determination they had!

SHOHRE (DUBAI)

I have been on tenterhooks since I started reading the story of this dog from Thailand. I am so pleased that it ended in such a good way. Top marks Bob for achieving what seemed an impossible situation.

KARL DEVRIES (NETHERLANDS)

What a lovely ending to Gypsy's story from a poor start in life. She deserves every happy moment with Bob from now on. May they have lots of good times together.

LYNN RAMSDEN (CANADA)

Very touching story which brought a few tears to my eyes. I am relieved that it ended so well. Such a lucky dog!

SUSAN POMFREY (ROTTERDAM)

I don't know how Sue kept it to herself for so long. What a magnificent end to your exciting story Bob! You deserve Knighthoods both of you!!

MARILYN KEANE (UK)

I read each instalment about Gypsy and was thrilled to know she got to England in the end after all that drama and stress.

BERNHARD GETZ (NORWAY)

Dear Sue. I have so enjoyed reading Bob's story about Gypsy and the exciting adventures they had. I think it deserves to be made into film! She is quite a determined four-legger and seems to have made a lasting impression on many people around the world as well as me!

ANTONETTE (BELGIUM)

I was so excited when I read that all your hard work had paid off and Gypsy will be in a loving home for many years, I hope.

ALBERT RICE (SARK)

I was so touched by this story as it unfolded and the outcome is just what I hoped for. It would make a lovely film!

ANOUK LAURENT (CANADA)

I knew Gypsy's story since before Bob offered to write it, but wasn't I tight lipped not to tell anyone about how her story ended! Thanks, Bob, for telling us this heart warming and beautifully written story of Gypsy...and of course for your perseverance to rescue her from thousands of miles away to give her a home. Not forgetting those kind people in the DRCS, Koh Samui working so hard to make life better for these silent creatures.

SUE GOKGOR (Editor of 'Friends of Doris Day')

I remained on the writing team for nearly four years and wrote other animal/travel and Doris Day-related articles till Sue stopped producing the three-times-per-year magazine due to ill health. It was comforting to know that this was always sent to Doris and was displayed on her coffee table for her visitors to read. I did eventually join the Doris Day Animal Foundation (DDAF) and it was exciting to occasionally receive letters written by Doris herself as well as the official newsletters. The last one I received from her was about a month before she passed away from pneumonia at the age of 97. She mentioned she was suffering with carpal tunnel syndrome at that time, making it difficult to write. Little did I know that the world of entertainment would soon lose one of the biggest stars ever in films and music. I was devastated, to put it mildly.

What a Coincidence!

'We realised we were only a few
feet away from Goldie Hawn!'

Strangely enough, at different points in my life, Doris has influenced certain aspects. When I was about 12 years old, I was taken to see the Alfred Hitchcock film 'The Man Who Knew Too Much.' It starred Doris and James Stewart and made a huge impression on me. Her biggest hit record was performed in it, called 'Que Sera, Sera,' which was number one in England for six weeks. Prior to seeing that, my first film starring Doris was 'Calamity Jane', a musical set in the Wild West. That was the start of my fan worship.

For those unfamiliar with Doris Day's career, in the late fifties and early sixties she was voted top box office star for six years and was more popular than Marilyn Monroe. She appeared with most of the major male stars of the period, like Rock Hudson, Cary Grant, James Cagney, and James Garner, in such films as 'Love Me or Leave Me', 'Pillow Talk', and 'Move Over Darling'. This was in addition to having a string of hit singles for about twenty years.

I happened to read in 2016 that it was sixty years since the Hitchcock thriller was released, so we thought it would be a good idea to visit Marrakech and see how much it had changed. By this time I had started writing articles for different magazines, so eventually I wrote an account of our adventures in Morocco. This included a trip up the Atlas Mountains in a taxi going from full sunshine to blizzards! It was so strange standing in a foot of snow wearing sandals, shorts, and t-shirts!

Our intention was to visit La Mamounia Hotel, where the projected filming was to take place. It was famous for celebrities like Marlene Dietrich, Freddie Mercury, Mick Jagger, and Sir Winston Churchill staying there. The latter used to paint the Atlas mountains when he was resident (on canvas, of course!). Due to refurbishment, filming was transferred to another hotel called La Menara, where Doris and the film crew actually stayed. We approached the security guards on duty outside but were denied entrance, and with them brandishing rifles, we decided not to be too insistent.

The main square, Jemaa el-Fnaa, was an interesting experience day and night. In the evening it was a vast open-air restaurant where you could watch rotating sheep's heads while they cooked. It was definitely not on our tasting schedule. One particular stall was devoted to selling false teeth, and in Arabic was a placard stating, 'Try Before You Buy.' There was never a queue forming there we noticed. There were amazing acts like fire eaters, jugglers, and snake charmers, but what freaked us out was the little Berber people, no more than four feet high. They watched everyone like hawks, and if they saw someone take a photo with them in it, they suddenly appeared in a flash with hands out for payment!

One annoying aspect when walking through the Souks was the stall holders pressurising people by asking which country they were from, like England, Spain, France and Italy. They spoke a limited vocabulary from those languages. I became increasingly perplexed by this attitude so I snapped one day and retorted, 'Reykjavik' to one guy. This struck him speechless, so that became the norm after that, and on other occasions we became Russian or Mongolian, and it worked every single time. That's a bit of friendly advice to anyone considering a trip to Morocco!

In Doris's book, Her Own Story, she expressed her concern over how donkeys were treated outside of those filming scenes. Unfortunately, back in the town we witnessed an awful sight. A cantering donkey passed us with its long tongue dangling down on one side, panting furiously as it dragged a large wooden container along, full of meat. Sad to say, in all those years, nothing had really altered. We instantly decided on reaching home to adopt a couple of donkeys, and I still do so to this day.

About five years after Gypsy's exodus from Thailand, we chose to take a holiday in Tossa del Mar on the Costa Brava, Spain. It was a quaint seaside town much quieter than the noisy neighbouring resort of Lloret de Mar. The most amazing coincidence occurred on our last day when we encountered the Bottles Bar. From outside we could see that its defining feature was a vast collection of huge posters plastered on the walls devoted to film and music icons.

I was naturally curious to see if there was one of Doris Day, and lo and behold, there she was right next to one of Elvis Presley in a scene from Jailhouse Rock. Doris's poster was a scene from Love Me or Leave Me, one of her more dramatic roles. I couldn't resist discussing her with Veronica, the lady who owned the bar, who actually hailed from Tewkesbury in England.

I mentioned about being a lifelong fan of Doris, which led on to what Doris was currently doing then with regard to animal welfare. Inevitably the subject of Gypsy entered the conversation and we just had to tell her the story. She looked quite emotional and told us she had inherited her two Alsatians from a nearby animal sanctuary run by a German lady called Ulrike, and her best friend was currently working there. I said that we knew someone called Ulrike with the surname Brentzel, in connection with the DRCS on Koh Samui.

She looked astonished and said she was sure it was the very same lady who had opened the rescue centre there just over two years ago! Ulrike had mentioned working in

Thailand when they first met. We could not believe what we had just heard!

"You have missed her by about an hour, as she calls in regularly to leave leaflets on my bar counter," she informed us. We were absolutely in shock at this revelation and very disappointed at the same time. Veronica said she would telephone her and ask her if she would come back and meet us. Unfortunately, it went straight to answerphone, so she left a message about us. We kept knocking back a few more beers for a couple of hours but had to leave eventually.

It was our last evening and we had arranged a final night out with friends from the hotel. We left our email address with Veronica for Ukrike to contact us, but for some reason she never got in touch. Maybe because she never received that note? We would have loved to have told her that Gypsy did get to England with her help! We suspect, though, that at some point Brigitte would have informed her of that.

We could not believe Doris Day had inadvertently led us into this bar, and the subsequent conversation about dogs linked us up with Ulrike again. We never went back to that area of Spain again, so we were never actually able to meet face to face, presuming it was the same woman. Latterly, she only ever made a few rare visits to Koh Samui, but never when we were there. While researching for this book, I discovered that Ulrike Brentzel is now connected to a dog rescue centre in Crete, so she is still very much involved with animal welfare, just in another place.

After deciding to have a holiday in Skiathos, Greece, we went online and discovered they had a dog sanctuary in the hills, and people could visit them and take dogs for walks. We did that a few times and also visited the Cat

Welfare shop on the edge of Skiathos town. Whilst there, we learnt that Goldie Hawn and Kurt Russell were regular visitors to the island, having friends who lived there.

One day, to our surprise, we realised that we were only a few feet away from Goldie in the sea on Mandraki beach. I had a marvellous conversation with her for about fifteen minutes, and she was a most natural, friendly person and so un-star-like.

At that time she had taken a break from making films and was promoting her charity in different countries regarding mental health concerning children (MindUP: The Goldie Hawn Foundation, founded in 2003). She only spoke briefly about her film career, and only because of questions we asked her. She subsequently returned to the big screen in 2017 with 'Snatched', which was fifteen years after her last film, 'The Banger Sisters.' Meeting such a fabulous lady was certainly a holiday event to remember!

Digressing just a little, on our travels we always seemed to get involved with animals in some way or another. One year we decided to go to Dubrovnik, Croatia, and booked self-catering in a rather splendid but expensive apartment with high ceilings. This was situated in the old town, inside the walls, on a side street up a few short flights of steps. We were taken aback as we neared the apartment when suddenly we spotted lots of tiny heads popping in and out of holes in the walls. It was a whole family of at least a dozen mostly ginger kittens, all barely three or four inches long. All of them miaowing together was considerably distressing when we passed them, as they were obviously very hungry. We were compelled immediately to go to the supermarket and buy tins of tuna, dry kitten food, milk, and small plastic bowls. We then placed separate bowls on the steps and watched them at feeding time. Thankfully, the mother eventually appeared, so the family was complete.

We did this throughout our holiday, and then it suddenly dawned on us that they were now accustomed to getting their daily meals. What would happen when we had returned home? Phil came up with the idea of leaving some food behind when we vacated the hotel, along with a note requesting the next occupants to continue to do the same as we had been doing. It was a shot in the dark but worth a try. Hopefully they were in the same mindset we were in, but of course we would never find out.

Back in 1978 I was invited over to Los Angeles to meet my favourite film and recording star, by the UK Doris Day Fan Club secretary, Sydney Wood. Doris had recently employed him as her 'house man' after both his parents were killed in a car accident. His job consisted of maintaining the grounds and other facilities and assisting with Doris's ever-expanding dog family.

I declined his invitation, unfortunately, due to my inherent fear of flying, and by the time I conquered it, Doris had left Los Angeles to live in Carmel, and I had lost touch with Sydney. This meant that the opportunity had long passed and I have regretted it ever since. Little did I know that many years later, Doris would feature in my life again with regard to Gypsy.

Come Fly with Me!

'A hand suddenly appeared
and snatched about fifty dollars!'

Despite being employed by a travel company sending clients all over Europe and the Caribbean by plane, I could not even contemplate going on a flight. All the foreign holidays I had taken by this time had been overland by train and coach and were considerably tiring. That was until 1983, when I was invited by Phil, who worked in Lunn Poly Travel, to go to Barbados for 12 days for a mere £112. I adamantly refused by lamely and stupidly saying, "But you can't get there overland!" However, my staff niggled away till I eventually gave in, thinking it was six months away and it would never materialise!

Each time I thought about this Caribbean holiday, I had severe panic attacks and my legs would feel completely numb. Someone informed me I could buy a cassette via mail order about conquering the fear of flying, so I decided it was at least worth trying. With trepidation, I thought it more than likely would not work. Lying spread-eagled on my bed, I had to imagine my right leg was made of orange jelly and concentrate on that till I felt totally relaxed. The same procedure with my left leg, then my arms, and in turn my whole body became what I could imagine as a giant jelly baby! I was then talked through arriving at the airport and checking in, followed by going through customs. So far so good.

The next section of this hypnotism course was to wander around the duty-free section and purchase goods. Unfortunately, by then I had gone into a deep sleep before I had even paid for the imaginary items I had bought! This happened on three occasions, which meant I never got to the point of climbing the plane steps and taking my seat, which was the main objective of the exercise. This caused me to abandon this procedure and I decided I would have to just take a chance on the day!

My next strategy was to visit my doctor, who prescribed a course of diazepam to be taken each time I became stressed out about the holiday. He did suggest an alternative option as well, and that was by risking a short flight. After much thought, I chose Majorca for seven days. After booking that for only £25 return after a staff discount, I was offered a free week in the Palma Nova Morokito apartments by a hotelier I was responsible for paying. That was the advantage of being in that job, but I never had enough holiday leave to accept very many 'freebies', unfortunately.

When the day arrived, a strange feeling of serenity overcame me, and without any tablets or alcohol, I was able to physically get past duty-free and board the plane. My prayers had been answered. I felt a slight apprehension when the flight was due to take off, but gritted my teeth and closed my eyes. When the plane levelled out, I opened them and glanced out of the window. Below I could see some land between the clouds, but straight ahead was a huge stretch of marshmallow-like terrain as far as the eye could see, topped with the bluest sky you could ever imagine.

What have I been missing all these years, I thought? I was elated at my achievement and at that moment my future holiday horizon expanded into cinemascope! At this time of writing, I estimate that I have flown on over five hundred planes, including forty-four to Amsterdam and twenty-eight to and within Thailand! Not bad for a late starter, and I have no intention of stopping just yet!

Having recently bought my first video camera before my first flight, I was so pleased that I had decided to take it with me to Majorca. With the captain's permission, next moment I found myself in the pilot's cabin filming the controls and part of the ongoing flight. Of course that would be out of the question nowadays because of the strict security surrounding air travel. I could not believe I had gone from being petrified to be in the air, to producing a film in the plane!

We became aware of a lady in the next aisle sobbing on her own. She said she was terrified as it was her first flight going to see her daughter, who was a hotel rep in Palma. I explained the problems I had endured leading up to this flight and she began to laugh. I definitely calmed her down, so we agreed to check in together when we returned home the following week so we could all sit together.

With that accomplishment, my trip to Barbados six weeks away became an exciting prospect, even though it took more than three times longer than to fly to Majorca. That time soon passed and all of a sudden, this challenge I was facing was staring me in the face! By then, the thought of an eight-hour flight was not as daunting, but I must confess to taking half a diazepam tablet in the airport, to be on the safe side. Phil was convinced I would suddenly change my mind at the last minute and disembark, so he had a whole one.

An hour into the flight, we enjoyed our usual couple of Jack Daniel's just to calm our nerves. However, suddenly an awful feeling of panic overtook me when we had been airborne for about seven hours. I noticed through my window that on the horizon there were black clouds and forked lightning. I was quite scared, but as we approached the island, the storm had thankfully moved on to somewhere else.

Landing in Barbados airport, we experienced a comforting waft of warm air on alighting from the plane. This long-awaited holiday was so different from anywhere else I had been and has paved the way to visiting well over sixty-five different countries since then, and I am still adding to the list!

Unfortunately, the experience was marred by a dangerous situation that arose halfway through our time there. Idyllic as it may seem, taking a holiday in Barbados has a dark side behind its exotic glamour. For most of the time it was wonderful, but being advised by the hotel that we should leave Bridgetown by 6pm was quite disappointing. Apparently, it was unsafe for foreigners to explore the town after dark. We were warned not to take watches or jewellery with us if we did decide to go there, which of course we did.

Because I was responsible in my job for paying all the hotels in the Caribbean for Arrowsmith's clients, we were wined and dined in several of them. It was a whirlwind of fine meals, wine, and rum with fabulous entertainment from bands like the Barbados Steel Orchestra and various reggae artists. Unfortunately, a very serious incident happened which changed our whole opinion of the island.

Some of the advice given by the Rockley Beach Hotel was to stay within their grounds unless booking an official trip to certain landmarks, like Bathsheba, Sam Lord's Castle, and Harrison's Cave in St. Thomas. I must point out that armed guards actually patrolled the perimeter of the hotel while the locals peered longingly through the fences.

We hated being restricted like that, so one evening we decided to risk venturing out to a restaurant called the Captain's Table, a short distance away. Feeling quite proud that we had 'escaped' the confines of the hotel, I was counting out some dollar notes we had left over outside the restaurant, when a hand suddenly appeared and snatched about fifty dollars! A tall, gangly young man ran away like a Harlem Globetrotter, with me in hot pursuit! Of course it was impossible to keep up with his speed, so I had to reluctantly grind to a halt! We did feel, though, that it was our own fault; we had been warned about local crime, and we had dared to thumb our noses at it. Of course Phil quite rightly said to me, 'Well, it was your idea, Bob!'

That was not the end of the story, though! Our hotel held weekend 'discos' and the locals were allowed to attend on Sunday free of charge. Lo and behold, our 'thief' brazenly turned up with a man and woman! I recognised him instantly and confronted him by prodding him in the ribs with my room key, but off he ran with his two friends. During my pursuit he picked up a huge boulder and threw it at me, which thankfully missed. Ironically, that was in a block entitled 'Peace!' That spoiled their evening out at least as they disappeared into the night, leaving us more than a little shaken up!

On the last full day of our holiday we were waiting on the beach to catch the courtesy bus back to the Rockley Beach Hotel for the last time. Suddenly I spotted this guy again who was no more than twenty, striding towards us and menacingly swinging a huge club-like plank. I told Phil to immediately go up to the bus and, if possible, tell someone but keep a watchful eye. I stood my ground and psychologically argued my way through this awful situation even though I was quaking inside.

I explained that our time in Barbados had been ruined by his actions, and on reaching England, I would make sure it became a news item within the travel industry. I told him that anything he did to me now was being closely watched and would be reported to the police, and a spell behind bars would not make his life any easier. To be honest, I felt quite sorry for him really, but I needed to tell him a few home truths.

I also explained that I did not want the money back because I sympathised with his problems regarding hardship and the general poverty within the local village communities. Gradually his face relaxed, and he said he was sorry for what he'd done and threw the plank down on the sand. We shook hands, and I wandered up to the bus quite happy at the outcome and also with a sense of relief! In a way it was worth going through this predicament in that far-off country. If I had not been persuaded to fly there in the first place, we might never have gone to Thailand and ultimately met Gypsy!

Ever since Gypsy was brought to England, family and friends have tried to persuade me to try and go on TV and tell her story. For instance, Paul O'Grady, Richard and Judy, and Sharon Osbourne were all dog lovers and hosted regular chat shows around that period. I never approached any of them, as the thought of sitting in front of TV cameras speaking to them about our incredible experience horrified me. As outgoing as I am, I am far more comfortable behind a camera! Strangely enough, I feel that I could cope with this scenario now, especially if I had a book to discuss, like this one, for example! (Maybe!)

Sadly, Gypsy had to be put to sleep in 2013, aged approximately fifteen, as she became too unsteady on her feet and lost a considerable amount of weight. It was the worst decision we had ever had to make, but we could not bear to see her suffering like that. Suddenly, 13 years of caring for her seemed as though that time had gone by in a flash. It was probably the most important and memorable phase in our lives, and we were comforted in knowing that we had given her the best life possible. If she had remained in Koh Samui, she would more than likely have had a much shorter life span.

After Gypsy's demise we were left with just two dogs...Bruno and Toby. Sadly, Bruno took ill and had to be put to sleep aged thirteen because of cancer. Two years later Toby became unwell, and we were reluctant to put him in kennels, so we decided to take him on his first official holiday with us to Scarborough. We stayed in the Royal Hotel, but he was a nightmare once we left him to have breakfast. He howled and barked until we returned, so for the remaining three days we had to eat separately! We enjoyed taking him to Robin Hood's Bay and Whitby, so it was a very different holiday for us, being used to flying everywhere abroad.

Sadly, soon after, Toby's health went downhill. First it became difficult for him to climb the stairs on his way to sleep on my bed. I decided to sleep downstairs on a spare single bed so it made it easier for him. Unfortunately, it got to the point where his back legs kept giving way until he could no longer walk or stand on them. It was time to make an excruciating decision and take him for the last time to the vet.

I have not considered owning another dog since, but that might change if I become unable to continue travelling abroad. I am hoping I have a few more years left to do that, as I still have nine years left on my passport!

For many years Phil and I have been working on this definitive story in stages, commencing with an original article about Gypsy which he submitted to the Kennel Club Gazette, a glossy magazine for breeders, in 1999. They accepted the article within a week, and he donated his fee of £200 to the DRCS. This only covered our first two visits to Thailand and our involvement with the beach dogs and meeting our beloved dog for the first time. It caused quite a reaction from some of the readers.

Some time later I decided to continue the story, and we pooled our different ideas and memories of the many adventures we had during the course of this life-changing period. Whilst concluding this story, I have realised that we actually met Gypsy for the first time just over 25 years ago. A quarter of a century later, here I am about to have it published.

Tragically, Phil had a series of major operations over a period of ten years, including a pancreatic operation, sepsis, a triple heart bypass, followed by a spinal operation, so everything went on hold for a while. For his last three years, Phil was coping with cancer (myeloma) and also had type 2 diabetes. Sadly, he passed away in March 2019 after only two days staying in a hospice.

No longer needing all the time I spent caring for him, once I had acclimatised myself to being alone after such a long, stressful time, I decided to resume my writing career.

I gradually began having my articles and poetry regularly accepted for publication by magazines like Best of British, Weekly News, the Oldie, This England, and several others. I also had poetry and an article published in the book 'People of Bollington' plus two scary true stories in the American magazine 'Paranormality.' This convinced me to persevere with my book, and I honestly feel that Phil is here, looking over my shoulder as I continue to finish creating this wonderful and unique account of Gypsy's journey and happy life in England.

One strange event coincided with my writing regarding an article I wrote about the record label Tamla Motown. In the sixties, when Motown launched their first tour of the UK in 1965, I excitedly booked to see it at the Liverpool Empire. I was only twenty-one at the time. Stevie Wonder, the Supremes, the Miracles, and Martha & the

Vandellas were the acts on stage, but amazingly the theatre was only about one third full!

A popular southerner called Georgie Fame was the bill-topper, having recently had some chart hits like 'Yeh, Yeh.' The London venue was full to capacity, but around the rest of the country it was considered a 'ghost tour'! To be honest, he was so totally in stark contrast to the Motown acts that this may have had an effect on its saleability elsewhere. I do remember a number of people walking out after the Motown first half, which left an even smaller audience while Georgie was on. The same happened in the City of Chester. Soon after the tour, a huge surge in popularity for the Motown label came when a TV special hosted by Dusty Springfield was aired, but it was just too late to promote the tour. Talk about bad timing!

I had my article published in the Best of British magazine, and a short while later I noticed an advert online requesting people who had attended those concerts to contact them, which I did. I was asked to forward a copy of said article, and eventually I had a telephone call from Wise Owl Films, based in Yorkshire. They had previously made documentaries on Bob Marley and Kurt Cobain and were now about to produce one on Motown for BBC2.

I was subsequently asked to attend an interview in Liverpool, all expenses paid, including overnight accommodation, and the result was I was included in the programme for about 6 minutes, along with two friends from the bands Arrival & Kokomo, Frank Collins and Carroll Carter. Shown on New Year's Day 2023, it was still available to watch on YouTube at the time of writing, called 'When Motown Came To Britain'.

For those of you who are unaware of where Bollington is, it is a very dog-friendly village on the outskirts of Macclesfield, Cheshire. It is perfect for hikers and walkers, being situated on the edge of Derbyshire, and is only a forty-minute drive into Manchester, or a twenty-minute train journey from Macclesfield.

All the pubs are havens for dogs, and Gypsy often took us to our local pubs. The Cotton Tree is just a few streets from my house and is one of the quaintest hostelries you can imagine. Successfully managed by Jayne, Christina and her sisters, it is quite compact and cosy with a beautiful beer garden. Perfect for those hot afternoons, which seem to be happening less often judging by recent summers. They host themed nights for special historical occasions and are unique in the services they offer. Where else can you top up your groceries and also choose 'old-fashioned sweets' from the many jars lined up on the corner shelves? All the canine customers are well catered for with dog treats stored in small chests of drawers around the pub.

The Poachers Inn is down a country lane about five minutes from the house. With it also being a restaurant, it is more spacious with a large beer garden adjacent to the fields and hilltop behind. I cannot believe that these were the two pubs we visited when first arriving in Bollington in 1989, which is now 35 years ago! Twice a month, the latter pub has always held quiz nights and we frequently took part in those, and I still do. Early in 2020, I learnt that the DRCS was finding it increasingly difficult to keep operating, mainly because Covid was preventing people travelling there on holiday. They lacked volunteers and experienced a huge reduction in donations due to insufficient tourists.

I arranged with Helen and Rob, the landlords at the Poachers, to host a quiz night specifically to raise funds for them. It was very successful with the regulars donating